RIBS, CHOPS, STEAKS & WINGS

Irresistible Recipes for the Grill,
Stovetop, and Oven

RIBS, CHOPS, STEAKS & WINGS

BY RAY "DR. BBQ" LAMPE

Photographs by Leigh Beisch

CHRONICLE BOOKS

SAN FRANCISCO

Library of Congress Cataloging-in-Publication Data available.

ISBN: 978-0-8118-6826-6

Manufactured in China.

Design by Katie Heit
Food styling by Sandra Cook
Prop styling by Sara Slavin
Typesetting by Janis Reed

The photographer wishes to thank her exceptional photo team. Thanks go to Sara Slavin for her incredible props and Sandra Cook for her inspired food and styling. Thank you to Penny Flood, Kate Robinson, and Sean Franzen for their support. Also, special thanks go to Vanessa Dina and Katie Heit for allowing me to be a part of another unbelievably wonderful project.

Big Green Egg all in one grill/smoker is a registered trademark of the Big Green Egg Company; Frank's Red Hot sauce is a registered trademark of Reckitt Benckiser; Gravy Master seasoning and browning sauce is a registered trademark of Gravymaster Inc.; Newman's Own marinara sauce is a registered trademark of Newman's Own Inc.; San Antonio Red chili powder is a registered trademark of Marshalls Creek Spices; Steen's Cane Syrup is a registered trademark of C. S. Steen's Syrup Mill, Inc.; Sugar In The Raw is a registered trademark of Cumberland Packing Corp.; Woodford Reserve distiller's select Kentucky Straight Bourbon Whiskey is a registered trademark of the Woodford Reserve Distillery.

10   9   8   7   6   5   4   3   2   1

Chronicle Books LLC
680 Second Street
San Francisco, California 94107

www.chroniclebooks.com

THIS BOOK IS DEDICATED TO MY SISTER DENISE.

ACKNOWLEDGMENTS

Thanks to Bill LeBlond for having the faith in me. Thanks to all the great people at Chronicle who turned my words into a beautiful book. Thanks to Scott Mendel for putting me in all the right places. Thanks to Judy for all the help at every turn. Thanks to Jim Nufer for believing in me.

TABLE OF CONTENTS

INTRODUCTION

THE CARNIVORE'S GUIDE TO THE UNIVERSE

Ribs, chops, steaks, and wings are the star attractions at any meal they are a part of. These are simply the most revered and tastiest parts of the cow, pig, and chicken. The back ribs, chops, and steaks all come from the highly prized loin area that is along the animal's back. The term "high on the hog" makes reference to this part of the animal as being reserved for those who are living well. I'll go along with that. The key is that these muscles don't have to work very hard in their first life so they produce tender and well-marbled meat in their second life as food. It's also quite well known among carnivores that meat from near the bone just plain tastes better, and cooking it while still on the bone adds even more flavor. So, the bit of hassle involved with eating a bone-in steak, chop, or rib is well worth it for the great taste. Clearly, this all applies to spare ribs in a big way, as well, even though they actually come from the side of the hog. The relationship between meat and bone is the secret to the amazing appeal of the barbecued rib in all its incarnations.

Then there's the wing. While it's not exactly high on the chicken, it sure doesn't get used much for flying by today's poultry and it's always served on the bone. (Stay away from anything called a boneless chicken wing or for that matter a boneless rib. What could those possibly be?) The chicken wing just might be nature's perfect food with all that delicious skin and the juicy tender meat. It just doesn't get any better. It's a great honor to write a book specifically about these cuts. I consider them to be the best meat products a cook can be given to work with and I'm happy to share my thoughts and recipes.

This isn't necessarily meant to be a grilling book, but since I am known as Dr. BBQ and since most of the favorite preparations of our four wonderful subjects involve grilling them, it's sort of got that feel to it. So I've included a grilling tutorial and an equipment primer to start the book, but your broiler or indoor grill or even a grill pan will work for many of the dishes. You'll just have to adapt the cooking times to your equipment and cook per the manufacturer's instructions. Even those of you cooking on the grill will have to adapt because every grill is a little different. But I suspect you've been practicing and are ready to get right at it with these new recipes.

Speaking of the recipes, I've covered some wonderful classic preparations for Ribs, Chops, Steaks, and Wings, such as New York Steak au Poivre and Grilled Veal Chops Oscar, but with a little of my own twist on them. I've also given you a few recipes specifically for cooking indoors because even I don't cook outside every day. I've included the recipe for the pan-fried sirloin that my grandma used to make so well and a really interesting combination of spare ribs and sauerkraut. I've even thrown in a couple of really unique ideas that you might not have expected such as the Seared Tuna Steaks with Wasabi Butter and the Turkey Wings Parmigiana. So let's get cooking. It's a carnivore's carnival.

GET COOKING

CHARCOAL OR GAS OR . . . ?

That is a question I am asked all the time, so it seems like a good place to start. I think we can all agree that there's no better way to cook ribs, chops, steaks, and wings than on the grill. They all benefit greatly from that smoky char that comes from a hot, open fire. But there are many types of grills, and the one you choose will have a great impact on the final outcome of your cooking. In my not-so-humble opinion on this subject, charcoal grills rule! The food just plain tastes better when cooked over charcoal. Burning whole logs of real wood can be equally good, but most of us don't have the kind of equipment to do it properly and in the wrong grill, an all-wood fire can create a taste that is just too smoky for most people. Most of the modern charcoal grills are very easy to use. They have tight-fitting lids that allow you to control the fire by controlling the oxygen that the fire gets. Open the vents and the fire grows; close them and it calms down. It's pretty simple to cook at the heat level you desire with a good charcoal grill.

Then of course there are the gas grills. They are wildly popular because of convenience, and most of them do what they promise, which is to sear the food nicely and create the "fat in the fire" taste that substitutes reasonably well for the wonderful taste of cooking with charcoal. Most have multiple burners so you can have a hot and a cool zone and they all have adjustable flames. Many also have a nice rotisserie option but we won't be using that for the ribs, chops, steaks, or wings that we're discussing in this book.

There are a couple of lesser-known options for grilling, as well. Electric grills have become popular due to many condo and balcony restrictions against open flames, but I've yet to try one that could compare to charcoal or gas. They typically don't get hot enough to sear the meat well, but if that's all you can use, go for it. Pellet-fired grills are another option and they have become more popular lately. They use 100 percent wood pellets that are typically made of by-product sawdust, which is a good thing. The pellets are automatically fed into the firepot, so these grills have great temperature control and they have that great wood taste. I like these a lot.

WHAT KIND OF GRILL?

Once you've decided on charcoal or gas, there are still many different styles and models of grills to choose from. In the charcoal category, the most common are the kettle-style grills made of steel. These work very well for grilling and are pretty reasonably priced. There are some very nice larger box-shaped charcoal grills on the market these days as well. Most of them are well made and have a nice feature where you can move the fire up and down. In the more exotic column are the big Santa Maria–style grills that are very popular in California. These grills typically have a big wheel that you turn to raise and lower the grill and they are usually capable of using real wood since they have no cover and plenty of airflow. You won't have very good control of the fire, but that's okay because you can easily raise and lower the cooking grate as needed. Last but not least is my favorite, the Big Green Egg. It's a ceramic grill that burns charcoal, and its versatility is like nothing else.

Gas grills come in even more variations than their charcoal cousins. For hot grilling, the ones that use infrared burners can't be beat. These are similar to the high-energy broilers that many of the big-name steakhouses use. They aren't the best choice for slowing it down, though, like we'll be doing in the ribs chapter. Traditional gas burners are better at slow cooking but don't get quite as hot as the infrared ones when it's searing time. The good news is that many of the gas-grill manufacturers offer combination grills that use some of each. Some even have a charcoal option. There are many grill choices and most of them perform very well after you learn how to use them properly.

CHARCOAL

There are two main kinds of charcoal that are readily available. The most common is the briquettes that we are all familiar with. They're nicely shaped, uniform little black pillows that are kind of hard to light but burn for a long time once they're going. A little bit of charcoal trivia: the briquettes that we're all so familiar with were actually invented by Henry Ford, the same man who started Ford Motor Company. Charcoal briquettes are a good source of fuel for grilling, but please, avoid the self-lighting ones at all costs. The taste of the lighting chemical will stay with them throughout the cooking process and that taste will transfer to the food.

The other readily available type of charcoal is called lump charcoal. It is essentially just charred pieces of wood. Depending on where it's made, the primary wood may be oak, hickory, mesquite, or, in some cases, exotic woods from other parts of the world. It will always be hardwood, though, and that's a good thing. The lump charcoal has gained a lot of popularity in recent years among grilling aficionados because it is made simply out of hardwood with no additives. It also lights easier than briquettes do, and creates very little ash. To learn more about lump charcoal, take a look at www.lump-charcoal.com.

The two types of charcoal are really interchangeable for use in most charcoal grills. Though you may be

more familiar with charcoal briquettes, I encourage you to give the lump a try, as well, then choose the one that works best for you.

LIGHTING THE CHARCOAL

Once you choose your charcoal, you'll need a plan to get it lit. I'd strongly advise against using liquid charcoal starter. It really doesn't work that well unless you use a lot of it and then it imparts the flavor into your food. There are some other options that work just as well without the side effect of the undesirable taste.

If you're using briquettes, a great way to start them is with a charcoal chimney. These look like big metal beer mugs and are readily available in the grilling department. You fill the chimney up with charcoal and use a couple sheets of crumpled-up newspaper underneath to start it. It's safe and convenient and does a good job. After about 10 minutes the charcoal will be red hot. Just dump it on top of some unlit charcoal in the grill, mix it all up, and you're ready to cook. The chimney works well for lump charcoal, too, but it's really not necessary. Lump charcoal lights really easily, so I prefer to use the commercially available fire starters that are made of sawdust and paraffin. You nestle a couple of them down into the lump charcoal and light the top edge. In just 7 to 8 minutes, the paraffin will be burned off, the lump charcoal will be lit, and you'll be ready to cook. There are also small alcohol-based starters that work equally well.

Last, but not least, is the old standby, the electric charcoal starter. These have been around for many years and they work well if you have a convenient outlet. You just nestle the starter down into the charcoal and plug it in. In 7 to 8 minutes the coals will be glowing and you'll be ready to cook.

As you can see, with these simple tools instead of the can of lighter fluid, you can easily, and cleanly, have a charcoal fire ready to cook in less than 10 minutes. I truly believe the taste of charcoal cooking is well worth the trouble.

TOOLS

There are a lot of fun tools on the market for grilling but I try to stay with the simple ones that make the food better. The gadget tools seem to end up on a shelf in the garage pretty quickly. Number one on my list is a good thermometer for taking the internal temp of the meat. There is absolutely no better way to tell when the food is cooked to proper doneness than by taking its temperature. A good-quality instant-read thermometer that you hold in your hand is a must. Another nice addition is a remote thermometer that has the readout on a little screen with a cable that goes into the grill and has a probe on the end. The probe goes into the thick part of the meat and stays there for the entire cook. These are best for bigger items but can be used successfully with thick steaks and chops as well.

I'd also recommend a sturdy set of grilling tools. These should be long enough to keep your hands out of the fire when maneuvering the food. They should include a pair of tongs, a knife, and a big spatula. Heavy gloves or those big silicone mitts help to keep your hands cool, too. I always keep a pair of those around.

Speaking of gloves, I use those latex surgical type gloves to keep my hands clean when handling the meat outside, but I also use them when I'm getting set up and handling charcoal and dirty grates. When you're done, just take them off and your hands are clean.

Lots of big platters are important, too. You must always use a new platter for the meat after it's cooked. You should *never* put the cooked meat back on the same platter without a thorough washing with hot soapy water. I like those silicone brushes for applying sauce on the grill. They look nice and clean up so easily. A dedicated sauce pan or bowl is a must so you don't ruin the fancy stuff from the kitchen. I often use disposable aluminum pans around the grill instead of bowls and indoor pans. Disposable is a good thing.

I also like to keep a selection of different wood chips on hand for those times that I want a little smoke flavor in my food. I often use a combination of a fruit-wood and a stronger smoke wood. I don't use wood all the time for steaks, but when I want a little change of pace, I do. I use wood chips fairly often for chops and wings, and always for ribs. Here are my favorite combinations for using wood chips when grilling.

DR. BBQ'S FOOD AND FAVORITE SMOKING WOOD PAIRINGS

Steaks	**Pork Ribs**
Oak	Cherry
Hickory*	Apple
Mesquite*	Pecan
	Oak
Pork Chops	Hickory*
Cherry	
Apple	**Wings**
Pecan	Cherry
	Apple
Lamb Chops	Hickory*
Wine Barrel Chips	
Grapevine	

These are the stronger smoke flavors and should be used in moderation.

RUBS AND SAUCES

The seasonings and sauces that you use are as important as any other aspect of the "day of cooking." But as I say in this book many times, there are no strict rules, except to cook what you like. I've given you some very good recipes for rubs and sauces in this book, but always remember that none of them is meant to be exclusively for that one dish they are listed with. You really should mix and match them and alter and twist them to your liking. I also know there are many great rubs and sauces being sold by some of the best cooks in the country, some you've heard of and others you haven't . . . just yet, anyway. I've given you some great sources for many grilling accessories at the back of the book, too, so look around and have fun experimenting.

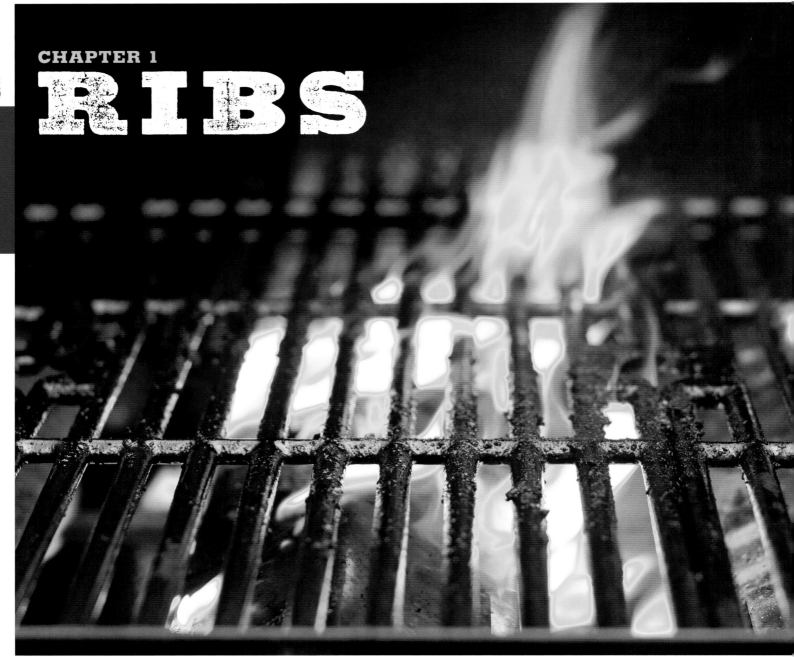

THERE IS SIMPLY NO OTHER FOOD THAT INSPIRES MORE PASSION AMONG FOODIES THAN RIBS. PEOPLE JUST LOVE TO EAT RIBS,

cook ribs, and even just talk about ribs. Ribs are mostly barbecued, of course, but even that single word brings about robust discussion and strong opinions. Beef ribs or pork ribs? If pork, should you use traditional spare ribs or the more luxurious baby back ribs for your barbecue? If you choose spare ribs, should you serve them whole or cut down to the St. Louis style? Maybe beef ribs would be better. Short ribs or beef back ribs? Should they be long bones or cut across the bones in the flanken style. You can even get short ribs in a boneless version in some stores. Why not have those?

RIBS RECIPES

Once you've decided which ribs to cook, you'll still have a long way to go before you get to eat. Should the membrane be removed from the back? Should you boil the ribs before cooking them? Will you use a simple salt-and-pepper seasoning or a complex barbecue rub? What kind of wood should you use? Will you wrap them in aluminum foil for part of the cooking to tenderize the ribs? What temp will you cook them at? Should you sauce the ribs while they're cooking? Should you serve sauce on the side? Or should you try those dry-rubbed ribs you've heard about?

These are all good and fair questions because ribs are an exciting and complicated subject. I'll try to cover as much as possible here, but, really, the best way to learn about ribs is to get cooking.

RIB CHOICES

I love beef ribs and they can be cooked in the barbecue pit very well, but for most of us barbecued ribs means pork. Pork ribs just seem to have the right amount of meat per bone and the right amount of marbling to cook beautifully on the grill or smoker. The taste of pork is just right with the barbecue flavors of a good rub mixed with a little smoke and glazed at the end with a tasty sauce. Beef ribs play a respectable second fiddle and I've given you some good recipes for them here, but when we're talking barbecued ribs it's really all about the pork. Pork ribs don't get a USDA grade for quality like beef does. The reality is, pork in America is almost

all good quality and consistent. There are, however, heritage breeds of pork showing up in the stores these days such as Berkshire and Duroc. These are similarly good quality but have a unique taste, look, and texture. It's about personal taste. Give them a try and see if you like them.

CUTS OF RIBS

Pork spare ribs are the original ribs. They come from the side of the hog and are part rib bone, part cartilage from the sternum of the hog. Historically, the side ribs weren't a desirable part of the hog and were left for the hired help to eat, thus the term "spare." When cooked whole, spare ribs take a long time to cook, and if not cooked properly they will be fatty and tough. Spare ribs are a little more trouble than the other choices, but when they're cooked right, they have more flavor than just about any part of the hog. When you serve spare ribs, you must always cut them apart individually for your guests.

St. Louis–cut spare ribs are a trimmed-down version of spare ribs that's easier to cook and eat. If you've ever eaten a whole spare rib you know that it has two distinct parts: the rib bone and the tip, which consists of cartilage that goes in a different direction than the rib bone. To make the spare ribs a little easier to eat, and to create a shorter and more consistent cook time, many cooks opt for the St. Louis cut. To do this, lay the slab of full spare ribs on a cutting board meaty-side down. By looking and feeling, find the line where the bones end and the cartilage begins. With a sharp knife, cut across the slab just above the bones, separating the St. Louis–cut ribs from the rib tips. That's it! You can cook the rib tips in a similar fashion to the ribs and serve them as well or use them to flavor soup, beans, or greens.

Pork loin baby back ribs are pork but they aren't actually from baby hogs. It is just a good name for a good rib. They cook a little faster than the spare ribs and you can give guests half racks without cutting the ribs individually—they look great served that way, and guests will easily be able to pull the bones apart themselves. Loin baby back ribs are cut from the bones of the loin where the pork chops and the center cut pork roast also come from. As loin baby back ribs have become popular, the bone-in pork roasts have become pretty hard to find because you can't get both out of the same side of a hog.

Country-style ribs are pork, too, and I've included a recipe for them here. They're good, but just a little different: Country ribs are cut from either the shoulder or the loin and they can vary widely depending on where you buy them. With a little practice these can be an economical alternative to the true ribs.

Beef ribs are very good, but they take a little longer to cook and they aren't as consistently available as pork ribs. Like all other beef, they are graded by the USDA, but it's highly unlikely that you'll find anything besides USDA Choice, which is fine. USDA Prime would be good but probably not worth the extra money for a cut like this. I've included two good recipes for the kind of beef ribs I typically see in the store: The long-bone beef back ribs, which don't generally have much meat on them and are kind of hard to eat; and the cross-cut short ribs, which cook quicker and are quite tasty. In the restaurant world you'll also see big meaty beef short ribs that are wonderful. But they rarely show up in the supermarket and they take a long time to cook. Grab them if you see them and use the back rib recipe—just add some time and cook until tender.

TRIMMING THE RIBS

The ribs we see in the store these days are trimmed pretty well. If you see any big pieces of fat on your ribs trim them off, but the long cooking process will render most of it anyway and the fat will help keep the meat moist. If you're cooking spare ribs or St. Louis cut, you'll want to remove the flap of meat that runs across the bone side of the ribs. It just won't cook the same as the ribs, but it does make a tasty treat for the cook so be sure to throw it in the grill or smoker. For all pork ribs and beef back ribs, peel the membrane on the bone side before cooking. This will allow the seasoning and smoke to better flavor the meat. The membrane also gets chewy during the cooking and that's a bad thing. The best way that I've found to remove the membrane is to loosen it on the surface of one of the flat bones by sliding a butter knife or some other dull tool under it and working the tool side to side and up and down until you can fit your finger under the membrane. Then, work your finger under the membrane and try to pull it off in one big sheet. It may be slippery, in which case use a paper towel to grab it and peel it away. If it tears, just get it started again and continue pulling until you have it all off. With a little practice, you'll be able to do this quickly and in one swift pull.

COOKING THE RIBS

To cook good barbecued ribs, you'll need to learn how to keep the temperature low in your grill or smoker; but most of the new grills and all smokers can do that pretty well. You'll also need to allow a few hours for cooking, but the results will be worth all the effort.

I like to use a sweet barbecue rub. For my smoke, I like cherry wood, but apple works pretty well, too. I usually don't baste my ribs while they're cooking. I've found that leaving the lid closed, rather than opening the lid repeatedly (and letting all the heat out) just to spritz a little liquid on the ribs, makes for better ribs because opening the lid causes temperature drops and spikes, which will dry the meat out no matter how much you spritz them. If you cook the ribs nice and slow they won't get dry. Speaking of not getting dry, I do usually wrap my ribs in aluminum foil for an hour or so in the middle of the cooking process. Not only does this help tenderize the ribs but it keeps the ribs from getting dry and hurries their cooking along. I feel that the optimum rib-cooking temp is 275 degrees F, although I occasionally vary just a little in some of my recipes. When I have friends over, I brush the ribs with sauce during the last 30 minutes of cooking, but if I'm cooking for myself, I

have them just with the dry rub and maybe a little bit of sauce on the side.

I like to cook ribs for family get-togethers or holiday parties with a lot of guests. For these larger gatherings, I use a rib rack instead of just laying the ribs flat on the cooking grate. The rib rack holds the ribs vertically with the bones pointing up and down and can usually accommodate 6 to 8 slabs of ribs in a grill space that would only fit 2 to 3 slabs if they were lying down flat. If you use a rib rack, don't forget to shuffle the ribs about halfway through the cooking because the slabs on the inside don't get as much heat and smoke as the slabs on the outside. You'll also need to add a little extra cooking time. I find that though there's a little more effort with the rack, the ribs cook similarly lying down flat. You'll just be able to feed more guests.

COOKING TIMES FOR RIBS

Following are some general cooking times, but they will always vary depending on the type of grill you have, the size and cut of the ribs you choose, and the degree of doneness that you like. The best way to test the ribs for doneness is to touch them. Squeeze the meat between the bones with your thumb and forefinger or push down on the top. The ribs should be very soft and collapse between your fingers. Another tried and true method is to poke down into the meat with a wooden toothpick. If the toothpick slides through like it's in soft butter, the ribs are very tender. These techniques require a little practice to get down pat, but once mastered you'll get the ribs done perfectly every time. If you like your ribs falling off the bone tender I'd suggest a little extra time in the aluminum foil; and if you like them a little chewy, cook them a little less. If you like your ribs a little crunchy and charred on the outside, give them a little extra time on the grill at the end while brushing them with sauce, and if you like the sauce on the side like I do, just give them a quick flip on the grill au naturel at the end.

Whole spare ribs:
4 pounds per slab and cooking at 275 degrees F
3 hours in the smoke
1½ hours wrapped in foil
30 minutes back on the grill unwrapped

St. Louis–cut spare ribs:
2½ pounds per slab and cooking at 275 degrees F
2½ hours in the smoke
1 hour wrapped in foil
20 minutes back on the grill unwrapped

Loin or baby back ribs:
2 pounds per slab and cooking at 275 degrees F
2 hours in the smoke
1 hour wrapped in foil
20 minutes back on the grill unwrapped

SEASONING AND SAUCING THE RIBS

Now that you have chosen the ribs you want to cook and you've come up with a cooking plan, you'll want to season the ribs to make them taste good. I've given you a very good rib rub below as a place to start. Like so many of my recipes, I encourage you to put your own

spin on it. If you like your rubs a little sweeter just add a little more sugar. Or less if you prefer. Many cooks like their rubs on the spicier side. If you're one of them, feel free to add more cayenne or some ground jalapeño, or whatever your heat of choice may be. The possibilities are endless. There are also many great barbecue rubs for sale commercially, and I encourage you to try some of them. But if you're just a salt-and-pepper cook, that's fine, too. The same goes for sauce. I've given you a few sauce recipes throughout this book. Feel free to mix and match them, doctor them up, or use your favorite that I may not even know about yet. With all of this knowledge you should now be able to create your own signature rib recipe and be the champion of your neighborhood.

RIB RUB #99
MAKES ABOUT 1½ CUPS

¾ cup Sugar In The Raw	1 tablespoon ground cumin
½ cup salt	1 tablespoon chili powder
¼ cup paprika	1 teaspoon dry mustard
2 tablespoons finely ground black pepper	1 teaspoon ground coriander
1 tablespoon granulated garlic	½ teaspoon cayenne pepper
1 tablespoon onion powder	½ teaspoon ground allspice

Combine all ingredients, mix well, and store in an airtight container.

BLUE RIBBON BARBECUE RIBS

SERVINGS

I call these ribs "Blue Ribbon" because the wrapping technique and the addition of the sugar, honey, and apple juice have won many a blue ribbon on the barbecue cook-off circuit. My old buddy Bill Milroy from Denton, Texas, who's been cooking in these contests since the 1970s, tells me he's the guy who first tried this, and I believe him. At least a few hundred of us are doing it nowadays, so I guess it was a good idea! Wrapping ribs in aluminum foil gets them tender, but it also keeps the ribs from getting dry and it hurries the cooking time a little. I think the sugar, honey, and apple juice just make them taste better and many a barbecue judge agrees with me. These would go very well served with baked beans and potato salad.

2 slabs St. Louis–style ribs or baby back ribs

¾ cup Rib Rub #99 (page 21)

¼ cup Sugar In The Raw

½ cup honey

Cayenne pepper, as needed

⅔ cup apple juice

2 cups your favorite barbecue sauce

❶ At least a half hour and up to 4 hours before you plan to cook the ribs, peel the membrane off the back of the ribs and trim any excessive fat. In a small bowl, combine the Rib Rub and the sugar. Season the ribs liberally on both sides with the rub mixture. Refrigerate. ❷ Prepare the grill for cooking over indirect heat at 300 degrees F using apple or cherry wood for flavor. Place the ribs directly on the cooking grate, meaty-side up. Cook for 1 hour. Flip and cook for another 30 minutes. Flip again and cook until they are nicely caramelized and golden brown, about another 30 minutes but may vary depending on your grill. Transfer to a platter. ❸ Lay out two big double-layered sheets of heavy-duty aluminum

continued on next page . . .

. . . continued

foil, each long enough to wrap a whole slab of the ribs. Transfer the ribs to the foil, meaty-side up. Drizzle half of the honey on each slab. Dust each slab with cayenne pepper. Fold the foil up around the ribs into a packet. Before sealing add half of the apple juice to the bottom of each packet. Seal the packets snugly, being careful not to puncture the foil with the rib bones. Return to the grill for 45 minutes to 1 hour to reach your desired degree of tenderness. The best way to determine the doneness is to open the foil after 45 minutes and feel the texture of the meat. It should be very tender.

Transfer the foil packets to a platter. Raise the temp of the grill to 400 degrees F. Remove the ribs from the foil and return to the cooking grate. Divide the barbecue sauce equally between two bowls, one for brushing on the ribs as they grill and one for serving at the table. Brush the ribs with the sauce and flip. Brush the other side and cook for 5 minutes. Flip again, brush, and cook for 5 minutes. Discard the sauce that you've been brushing with. Remove the ribs to a platter. Serve ½ slab to each guest with the second bowl of sauce on the side.

SWEET-AND-STICKY BABY BACK RIBS

SERVINGS

Most people like their ribs to be on the sweet side with some sugar in the rub and a sweet barbecue sauce either used to baste the ribs while they cook or served on the side, or maybe even both. But others like their ribs to be over-the-top sweet, sticky, and gooey. Well these ribs are for those folks. I often use Sugar In The Raw, honey, molasses, or cane syrup to sweeten things up, but this recipe uses them all and it's quite a combination. Steen's is a brand name of cane syrup (as in "sugarcane") that's easily found in the South in either a glass bottle or a can. If you can't find it, you can order it online; if all else fails you can substitute maple syrup or additional molasses. These would go very well served with baked beans and corn pudding.

2 slabs pork loin baby back ribs, about 2¼ pounds each

Rib Rub #99 (page 21), as needed

·····

SWEET AND STICKY SAUCE
½ cup your favorite barbecue sauce

¼ cup Sugar In The Raw

¼ cup honey

¼ cup molasses

¼ cup Steen's Cane Syrup

¼ cup cider vinegar

1 tablespoon Louisiana hot sauce

❶ At least a half hour and up to 4 hours before you plan to cook the ribs, peel the membrane off the back of the ribs and trim any excessive fat. Season the ribs liberally on both sides with the Rib Rub. Refrigerate. ❷ To make the sauce: In a medium saucepan over low heat, heat the barbecue sauce. Add the sugar and mix well. Cook for 1 minute, until the sugar dissolves. Add the honey, molasses, cane syrup, vinegar, and hot sauce. Mix well and cook for 3 minutes, stirring often. Divide the glaze equally between two bowls, one for brushing on the ribs as they grill and one for serving at the table. Set aside.

continued on next page . . .

. . . continued

❸ Prepare the grill for cooking over indirect heat at 300 degrees F using apple or cherry wood for flavor. Place the ribs on the cooking grate, meaty-side up. Cook for 1 hour. Flip and cook for another 30 minutes. Flip again and cook until they are nicely caramelized and golden brown, about another 30 minutes but may vary depending on your grill. Transfer the ribs to a platter.

❹ Lay out two big double-layered sheets of heavy-duty aluminum foil, each long enough to wrap a whole slab of the ribs. Transfer the ribs to the foil, meaty-side up. Fold the foil up around the ribs into a packet. Seal the packets snugly, being careful not to puncture the foil with the rib bones. Return to the grill for 45 minutes to 1 hour to reach your desired degree of tenderness. The best way to determine the doneness is to open the foil after 45 minutes and feel the texture of the meat. It should be very tender. Transfer the foil packets to a platter. Raise the temp of the grill to 400 degrees F. Remove the ribs from the foil and return to the cooking grate. Brush with the glaze and flip. Brush the other side and cook for 5 minutes. Flip again, brush, and cook for 5 minutes. Discard the glaze that you've been brushing with. Remove the ribs to a platter. Serve ½ slab to each guest with the second bowl of glaze on the side.

APRICOT-GLAZED BABY BACK RIBS

4

SERVINGS

I've always liked savory dishes with the taste of apricot, and pork is the best fit of all. I first tried this technique with peach preserves, and you could certainly substitute that here. But I like the subtlety of the apricot even better. The combination of the sweet preserves with the salty soy sauce and the tangy hot sauce is great. When you add the distinct flavor of the Worcestershire, and then cut it all with your favorite barbecue sauce, well, you end up with some unique and fabulous ribs. I call for your favorite barbecue sauce in this recipe. You can use any of the barbecue sauces from within the book, a favorite bottled sauce, or your own secret recipe. These would go very well served with a baked sweet potato and creamy coleslaw.

2 slabs pork loin baby back ribs, about 2 ¼ pounds each

Rib Rub #99 (page 21), as needed

· · · · ·

APRICOT GLAZE

1 cup apricot preserves

½ cup your favorite barbecue sauce

1 tablespoon soy sauce

1 tablespoon Worcestershire sauce

1 tablespoon hot sauce

❶ At least a half hour and up to 4 hours before you plan to cook the ribs, peel the membrane off the back of the ribs and trim any excessive fat. Season the ribs liberally on both sides with the Rib Rub. Refrigerate. ❷ To make the glaze: In a medium saucepan over medium heat, melt the preserves. When the preserves are soft, add the barbecue, soy, Worcestershire, and hot sauces. Mix well and cook for about 3 minutes, until warm and well blended. Divide the glaze equally between two bowls, one for brushing on the ribs as they grill and one for serving at the table. Set aside. ❸ Prepare the grill or smoker for cooking over indirect heat at 300 degrees F using apple or cherry wood for flavor. Place the ribs directly on the cooking grate, meaty-side up. Cook for 1 hour. Flip and cook for another 30 minutes. Flip again and cook until they are nicely caramelized and golden brown, about another 30 minutes but may vary depending on your grill. Transfer the ribs to a platter. ❹ Lay out two big double-layered sheets of heavy-duty aluminum foil, each long enough to wrap a whole slab of the ribs. Transfer the ribs to the foil, meaty-side up. Fold the foil up around the ribs into a packet. Seal the packets snugly, being careful not to puncture the foil with the rib bones. Return to the grill or smoker for 45 minutes to 1 hour to reach your desired degree of tenderness. The best way to determine the doneness is to open the foil after 45 minutes and feel the texture of the meat. It should be very tender. Transfer the foil packets to a platter. Raise the temp of the grill to 400 degrees F. Remove the ribs from the foil and return to the cooking grate. Brush with the glaze and flip. Brush the other side and cook for 5 minutes. Flip again, brush, and cook for 5 minutes. Discard the glaze that you've been brushing with. Remove the ribs to a platter. Serve ½ slab to each guest with the second bowl of the glaze on the side.

MEMPHIS DRY-RUBBED BACK RIBS

4
SERVINGS

When you go to the barbecue joints in Memphis, you can typically get your ribs wet or dry, the difference being that the wet ribs will be finished with a pretty heavy slather of a tomato-based, fairly sweet barbecue sauce, while the dry ribs will be finished with an additional dusting of the house barbecue rub. I happen to like the dry-rubbed version better, but there's usually a bottle of sauce on the table so I can add a little if I want. The most famous of all the dry rib joints in Memphis is The Rendezvous and I really like their ribs. They use loin baby back ribs and they cook them over charcoal until done, then they finish them with another layer of their delicious dry rub. I hope you like my version. These would go very well served with white beans and cornbread.

2 slabs pork loin baby back ribs, about 2¼ pounds each	Rib Rub #99 (page 21), as needed

❶ At least a half hour and up to 4 hours before you plan to cook the ribs, peel the membrane off the back of the ribs and trim any excessive fat. Season the ribs liberally on both sides with the Rib Rub. Refrigerate. ❷ Prepare the grill for cooking over indirect heat at 300 degrees F using apple or cherry wood for flavor. Place the ribs directly on the cooking grate, meaty-side up. Cook for 1 hour. Flip and cook for another 30 minutes. Flip again and cook until they are nicely caramelized and golden brown, about another 30 minutes but may vary depending on your grill. Transfer the ribs to a platter. ❸ Lay out two big double-layered sheets of heavy-duty aluminum foil, each big enough to wrap a whole slab of the ribs. Transfer the ribs to the foil, meaty-side up. Fold the foil up around the ribs into a packet. Seal the packets snugly, being careful not to puncture the foil with the rib bones. Return to the grill for 45 minutes to 1 hour to reach your desired degree of tenderness. The best way to determine the doneness is to open the foil after 45 minutes and feel the texture of the meat. It should be very tender. Transfer the foil packets to a platter. Raise the temp of the grill to 400 degrees F. Remove the ribs from the foil and return to the cooking grate. Sprinkle lightly with additional Rib Rub #99. Cook for 5 minutes. Flip and sprinkle the other side lightly with the Rib Rub and cook for 5 minutes. Flip one last time and cook for 5 minutes more. Remove the ribs to a platter. Serve ½ slab to each guest.

OLD-SCHOOL SOUTHERN BARBECUED SPARE RIBS

SERVINGS

Barbecue ribs have changed a lot in the 25 years I've been cooking them. Complex barbecue rubs consisting of salt, sugars, spices, and herbs are very common these days as seasoning for ribs. Barbecue cookers with great temperature control make it unnecessary to baste or "mop" the meat, and barbecue sauce has become as popular as ketchup. We all used to cook whole spare ribs, too, but now we cut them so that they cook more evenly, or we cook the fancier loin baby back ribs. This is all well and good, but sometimes I feel like cooking some old-school ribs, so here is my delicious version. The flavors are simple and the meat may not be falling-off-the-bone tender, but these ribs are mighty good and you'll be enjoying a little of the roots of barbecue. These would go very well served with potato salad and collard greens.

2 slabs whole spare ribs, about 4 pounds each

1½ tablespoons salt

½ tablespoon finely ground black pepper

½ tablespoon granulated garlic

½ tablespoon onion powder

• • • • •

MOP
¼ cup olive oil

1 small onion, finely chopped

2 cloves garlic, crushed

1 serrano chile, seeded and finely chopped

¾ cup apple juice

¼ cup cider vinegar

¼ cup ketchup

2 tablespoons Worcestershire sauce

2 tablespoons soy sauce

2 tablespoons hot sauce

❶ At least a half hour and up to 4 hours before you plan to cook the ribs, peel the membrane off the back of the ribs and cut the flap off. Trim any excessive fat. Combine the salt, pepper, granulated garlic, and onion powder in a small bowl. Mix well. Season the ribs on both sides with the mixture. Refrigerate. ❷ To make the mop: In a medium saucepan over medium heat, heat the oil. Add the onion, garlic, and chile. Cook for about 4 minutes, stirring often, until the onion is soft. Add the apple juice,

continued on page 34 . . .

. . . continued

vinegar, ketchup, and Worcestershire sauce, soy sauce, and hot sauce. Mix well and cook for 10 minutes, stirring occasionally. Let rest for 15 minutes to steep. Strain the mop mixture through cheesecloth or a small strainer, then transfer to a spray or squeeze bottle. Set aside.

❸ Prepare the grill for cooking over indirect heat at 250 degrees F using hickory and cherry wood for flavor. Place the ribs, meaty-side up, directly on the cooking grate and close the lid. Cook for 1½ hours without opening the lid. Spray or drizzle some of the mop on the ribs and cook for another 30 minutes. Spray or drizzle more of the mop, flip, and spray or drizzle again. Repeat every 30 minutes until the ribs are tender. This should take 5 to 6 hours total. Check for doneness by sticking a toothpick down into the meat, between the bones. It should slide in easily. Transfer the ribs, meaty-side down, to a cutting board. With a sharp knife, cut through the slab completely at each rib. Flip the ribs back over and transfer them to a platter.

SPARE RIBS WITH GWYNETH'S RED CHILE BARBECUE SAUCE

SERVINGS

One of my many jobs is writing the "Ask Dr. BBQ" column for *Fiery Foods & BBQ* magazine and their accompanying Web site, Fiery-foods.com. I travel to Albuquerque a couple times a year to see the founder, and my mentor, Dave DeWitt. I've become very fond of the food of New Mexico so I wanted to include a recipe here for ribs with a red chile barbecue sauce. Who better to ask for help with that than Gwyneth Doland, the editor of the magazine. Gwyneth is an adorable young lady with a ton of talent and I think you're going to be hearing a lot from her in the future. Gwyneth created this sauce for me and here's what she has to say about it: "This barbecue sauce gets its smoky, earthy flavor from dried red chile pods. It calls for mild New Mexico and ancho chiles, but if you like a spicier sauce, try substituting some pasillas or a couple of dried chipotles." Look for the dried chiles in the Mexican foods section of your supermarket and online. These would go very well served with rice and pinto beans.

---

2 slabs whole spare ribs, about 4 pounds each

Rib Rub #99 (page 21), as needed

• • • • •

GWYNETH'S RED CHILE BARBECUE SAUCE
9 mild dried red New Mexico chiles

3 dried ancho chiles

1 tablespoon vegetable oil

2 cloves garlic, minced

1 small onion, finely diced

1 cup ketchup

¾ cup cider vinegar

½ cup molasses

½ cup honey

---

❶ At least a half hour and up to 4 hours before you plan to cook the ribs, peel the membrane off the back of the ribs and cut the flap off. Trim any excessive fat. Season the ribs liberally on both sides with the Rib Rub. Refrigerate. ❷ To make the barbecue sauce: Heat a cast-iron skillet over medium heat and toast the chiles on both sides until they soften slightly and become aromatic. Remove from the pan and tear the stems from the chiles. Pour out the seeds and discard the stems and seeds. Put the toasted chiles in a medium, heat-safe

continued on next page . . .

. . . continued

bowl and add enough hot water to cover. Keep the chiles submerged with a small plate or saucer. Let soak for 1 hour. Use tongs to transfer the chiles to a blender and purée, adding about 1 cup of the soaking water to make a thick sauce. Press the mixture through a fine-meshed sieve set over a large bowl. Set aside. In a medium saucepan over medium heat, heat the oil. Add the garlic and onion and cook for 5 minutes, until softened and pale gold. Add the strained chile purée, the ketchup, cider vinegar, molasses, and honey. Mix well. Bring to a boil, then reduce the heat and simmer for 5 minutes. Divide equally between two bowls and set aside. ❸ Prepare the grill for cooking over indirect heat at 275 degrees F using apple or cherry wood for flavor. Place the ribs, meaty-side up, directly on the cooking grate and close the lid. Cook the ribs for 2 hours. Flip and cook for another 30 minutes. Transfer to a platter. ❹ Lay out two big double-layered sheets of heavy-duty aluminum foil, each

long enough to wrap a whole slab of the ribs. Transfer the ribs to the foil, meaty-side up. Fold the foil up around the ribs into a packet. Seal the packets snugly, being careful not to puncture the foil with the bones. Return to the grill for 1 hour. Transfer the foil packets to a platter. Remove the ribs from the foil and return to the cooking grate. Cook for 30 minutes, then flip and spoon ½ cup of the sauce on the bone side of each slab of ribs, spreading it evenly to cover the ribs. Cook for another 30 minutes and flip again. Top each slab with another ½ cup of the sauce and cook for about another 30 minutes or to your desired degree of doneness. Check for doneness by sticking a toothpick down into the meat, between the bones. It should slide in easily. Transfer the ribs, meaty-side down, to a cutting board. With a sharp knife, cut through the slab completely at each rib. Flip the ribs back over and transfer to a platter. Serve with the remaining sauce on the side.

MOM'S PINEAPPLE TERIYAKI SPARE RIBS

SERVINGS

One of my earliest barbecue rib memories is of my mom cooking for all of her friends at a big party each summer at my grandma's house in Wisconsin. My mom's signature dish for this party was barbecued ribs that she cooked with an intensely flavored combination of crushed pineapple, molasses, and barbecue sauce. She would spend the whole day nurturing the ribs while her friends gathered around to have a few drinks and watch her work. I was young but I remember the guests' anticipation and how they loved her ribs, so I decided to re-create the recipe here. I think she'd be happy with my rendition. My mom didn't cook much barbecue, but when she did, it was something special. I'm proud to be able to share this recipe. These would go very well served with a rice pilaf and grilled pineapple slices.

2 slabs whole spare ribs, about 4 pounds each

Rib Rub #99 (page 21), as needed

• • • • •

PINEAPPLE TERIYAKI SAUCE
One 20-ounce can crushed pineapple, with the juice

1 cup molasses

½ cup your favorite barbecue sauce

¼ cup soy sauce

¼ cup rice vinegar

Juice of 1 lemon

1 teaspoon finely ground black pepper

❶ At least a half hour and up to 4 hours before you plan to cook the ribs, peel the membrane off the back of the ribs and cut the flap off. Trim any excessive fat. Season the ribs liberally on both sides with the Rib Rub. Refrigerate. ❷ To make the teriyaki sauce: Put the pineapple and the juice in a medium saucepan over medium heat. Add the molasses, barbecue sauce, soy sauce, vinegar, lemon juice, and pepper. Mix well and bring to a simmer. Cook for 2 minutes, stirring often. Transfer

continued on next page . . .

. . . continued

to a bowl and set aside. ❸ Prepare the grill for cooking over indirect heat at 275 degrees F using apple or cherry wood for flavor. Place the ribs, meaty-side up, directly on the cooking grate and close the lid. Cook the ribs for 2 hours. Flip and cook for another 30 minutes. Transfer to a platter. ❹ Lay out two big double-layered sheets of heavy-duty aluminum foil, each long enough to wrap a whole slab of ribs. Transfer the ribs to the foil, meaty-side up. Top each slab of ribs with one-fourth of the sauce, spreading it to cover the entire slab. Fold the foil up around the ribs into a packet. Seal the packets snugly, being careful not to puncture the foil with the bones. Return to the grill for 1 hour. Transfer the foil packets to a platter. Remove the ribs from the foil and return to the cooking grate. Cook for 30 minutes, then flip, and spoon ½ cup of the sauce on the bone side of the ribs, spreading it evenly to cover the ribs. Cook for another 30 minutes and flip again. Top with the remaining sauce and cook for about another 30 minutes or to your desired degree of doneness. Check for doneness by sticking a toothpick down into the meat, between the bones. It should slide in easily. Transfer the ribs, meaty-side down, to a cutting board. With a sharp knife, cut through the slab completely at each rib. Flip the ribs back over and transfer them to a platter.

SPARE RIBS COOKED WITH SAUERKRAUT

SERVINGS

Even in the case of ribs, man cannot live on barbecue alone. So I present another of my favorite family recipes. My mom and grandma loved to make spare ribs with sauerkraut. My grandma would cook the ribs in the kraut all day with onions and potatoes and sometimes even add a little barley. Be careful if you add barley because it will soak up a lot of juice and grow. Spare ribs are really overlooked as a great meat for soups, stews, and casseroles because we always think of them as strictly a barbecue dish. I believe this dish will convince you to consider them in other ways in the future.

SAUERKRAUT
Two 27-ounce cans sauerkraut, drained

1 medium onion, chopped

1 tablespoon caraway seeds

½ teaspoon sugar

½ teaspoon granulated garlic

½ teaspoon finely ground black pepper

3 cups peeled and diced russet potatoes

1 slab whole spare ribs, about 4 pounds

Salt and pepper, as needed

❶ Preheat the oven to 350 degrees F. To make the sauerkraut: In a large bowl, combine the canned sauerkraut, onion, caraway seeds, sugar, granulated garlic, and pepper. Toss to mix well. Spread the sauerkraut evenly in a 9-x-13-inch pan. Spread the potatoes evenly on top of the sauerkraut. **❷** Peel the membrane off the back of the ribs. Cut the ribs into 4 serving-size pieces. Season the ribs liberally on both sides with the salt and pepper. Place the ribs on top of the potatoes, overlapping as needed, trying to cover the entire surface of the potatoes. Cover the whole pan tightly with foil. **❸** Place in the oven and bake for 1½ hours. Remove the foil. There should be a little bit of liquid in the bottom of the pan. Add some water, if needed. Return to the oven and cook uncovered for 1 more hour, or until the ribs are golden brown and tender. To serve, put a portion of the ribs on each plate with a big scoop of the sauerkraut and potatoes on the side.

GRILLED COUNTRY RIBS WITH SAUTÉED APPLES

SERVINGS

Country-style ribs are a little different than loin baby back or spare ribs, but they're always pork. The original cut called "country-style ribs" came from the last 3 or 4 rib bones at the end of the pork loin. They were butterflied, kind of like a split pork chop. But as consumer preferences change, so do the options in the meat case. The butcher can't cut a full slab of loin back ribs and those 3 or 4 country ribs out of the same side of a hog, and the back ribs are very popular so you won't find the original country ribs very often anymore. But there is another part of the hog that gets packaged and sold as country-style ribs and they're pretty good, too. It's actually a slice of the shoulder that has a piece of the blade bone in it, and it kind of looks like a rib. This new cut is much more popular these days and can be cooked in about the same way. It may be a little denser and therefore a little chewier but, nonetheless, some good eating. I've paired these grilled country-style ribs with homemade sautéed apples, and it's a winning combination. These would go very well served with hash browns.

APPLES
4 large Rome apples

½ stick butter

½ cup brown sugar

2 teaspoons ground cinnamon

¼ teaspoon salt

▪ ▪ ▪ ▪ ▪

8 country-style ribs

Rib Rub #99 (page 21), as needed

❶ To make the apples: Core the apples and cut them into ½-inch cubes, leaving the skin on. In a large skillet over medium heat, melt the butter. Add the apples and cook for 5 minutes, stirring often. Add the brown sugar, cinnamon, and salt, and mix well. Cook for another 15 minutes, stirring often, until the apples are soft. Set aside and keep warm. ❷ Season the ribs liberally on both sides with the Rib Rub. ❸ Prepare the grill for cooking over direct medium heat. Place the ribs directly on the cooking grate. Cook the ribs for 4 minutes. Flip and cook for another 4 minutes. Flip again and cook for another 3 minutes. Flip one final time and cook for another 3 minutes or to your desired degree of doneness. Remove to a platter and let rest for 5 minutes. Add the warm apples to the platter to serve.

BEEF SHORT RIBS WITH ZINFANDEL SAUCE

4
SERVINGS

Beef ribs are different than pork ribs, just by nature of the size and the texture of the meat. A full slab of beef ribs would feed quite a few people, it wouldn't fit on your plate, and it would take a really long time to cook—even by barbecue standards. So they're usually cut, cooked, and served a little differently than pork ribs. For this recipe, I've used short ribs that are cut across the bones, creating a small enough piece of meat to cook fairly quickly. This type of cut also allows for a lot of surface for glazing, so I've made a sauce using reduced Zinfandel. I love the Zins from California with grilled and smoked food and these beef ribs are a great match. Be sure to get an extra bottle of the Zin for drinking with your ribs. These would go very well served with buttered noodles and grilled asparagus.

ZINFANDEL SAUCE
2 cups good-quality
Sonoma Zinfandel

3 tablespoons butter

1 small red onion, chopped

1 clove garlic, crushed

2 tablespoons flour

2 cups low-sodium beef
broth

▪ ▪ ▪ ▪ ▪

4 pounds cross-cut beef
short ribs, ½ inch thick

Steak Seasoning Salt
(page 82), as needed

❶ To make the sauce: In a medium saucepan over medium heat, heat the Zinfandel. Bring to a simmer and cook for about 15 minutes, until reduced by half. Remove from the heat and set aside. In another medium saucepan over medium heat, melt the butter. Add the onion and garlic and cook for about 4 minutes, stirring often until the onion is tender. Add the flour and mix well until blended. Add the beef broth and the reduced Zinfandel and mix well. Bring to a simmer and cook for about 10 minutes, until thickened.
❷ Prepare the grill for cooking over direct medium heat. Season the ribs on both sides with the Steak Seasoning Salt. Place the ribs directly on the cooking grate. Cook for 5 minutes. Flip and brush with the sauce. Cook for another 5 minutes and repeat. Continue flipping and brushing for about 40 minutes, until the ribs are browned and tender. Discard any remaining sauce. Remove to a platter to serve.

BARBECUED BEEF BACK RIBS

4

SERVINGS

You'll usually see beef back ribs in 4- to 6-bone pieces and they typically don't have much meat on them. These are the bones that the rib roast or rib-eye steaks come off of, so you'll often see them in abundance around Christmas and New Year's when people are buying a lot of rib roasts. They're usually pretty cheap, and that's a good thing because, like I said, there just isn't much meat on them. The meat needs a lot of cooking to make it tender, but when it's cooked right, it's really good meat, so it's worth the effort. You'll need at least a pound of meat per person, or 2 to 3 bones. Wrapping these in foil is essential to get them tender. If you're the adventurous type, add a half cup of strong coffee to the package when you wrap the ribs. I think you'll find it to be a pleasant surprise. These would go very well served with baked beans and potato salad.

5 pounds beef back ribs,
Rib Rub #99 (page 21), as needed

2 cups your favorite barbecue sauce

❶ Peel the membrane off the back of the ribs. Season the ribs liberally on both sides with the Rib Rub. ❷ Prepare the grill for cooking over indirect heat at 250 degrees F using oak or hickory wood for flavor. Place the ribs, meaty-side up, directly on the cooking grate. Cook for 2½ hours. Flip the ribs and cook for 30 minutes. Lay out a big double-layered sheet of heavy-duty aluminum foil and place the ribs on it, meaty-side up. Wrap up the ribs, sealing the package tightly. Return the ribs to the grill for 1 hour. Transfer the packet of ribs to a platter. Raise the temp of the grill to 400 degrees F. Remove the ribs from the foil and return to the cooking grate. Brush with the sauce. Cook for 15 minutes, flip the ribs, and brush again. Repeat once more. Remove the ribs to a platter and serve with additional barbecue sauce on the side.

CHAPTER 2

CHOPS

CHOPS ARE THE LITTLE BROTHERS OF STEAKS. THE CUTS ARE VERY SIMILAR TO THOSE OF STEAKS, BUT THE ANIMAL OF CHOICE DIFFERS.

Steaks are generally cuts of beef, while chops are generally cuts of pork, lamb, or veal. In the United States, pork chops are by far the most popular. While they are usually a little cheaper than steaks, properly cooked, pork chops are every bit as good. We love them fried, smoked, broiled, braised, and grilled. But grilling is our favorite way to cook our chops, and rightfully so. Grilling a pork chop gives it a crispy caramel crust on the outside that is a wonderful companion to the tender and juicy "other white meat" on the inside. Nowadays, we can even serve them a little bit pink on the inside, making them extra tender and juicy. Today's pork is safe to eat like that and many of us have embraced

CHOPS RECIPES

the idea. I know I sure have. In this chapter, you'll find some fun and interesting recipes using all the cuts of pork chop. But I've also given you a wonderful recipe for double-thick lamb chops and another for grilled veal chops served in the barbecue version of the classic Oscar presentation.

CHOP CHOICES

The choices aren't quite as varied as they are in steaks, but there are definitely different types of pork chops to consider. Pork chops are all cut from the loin area, which runs along the back of the hog and is historically considered to be the best part of the hog. The chops cut from the loin vary quite a bit in shape and texture. I've listed the common names for the cuts, but many markets customize these terms, so you may have to have a little local knowledge to get the right chops. The good news is that all the cuts of pork chops cook the same and they're pretty much interchangeable in the recipes. All of the pork-chop cuts are available with the bone in or boneless. I always prefer to cook them on the bone because, as any serious carnivore will tell you, they just taste better that way. But the boneless ones sure do look nice and many guests find it easier to eat them, so I use them as well. The choices of lamb and veal chops are very similar but you rarely see them boneless.

CUTS OF CHOPS

The rib chop comes from the front and center part of the loin and utilizes the same bones as loin baby back ribs. The meat is tender and juicy and resembles a rib-eye steak. You'll find these in both the bone-in and the boneless variety. Rib chops are best cut ¾ to 1¼ inches thick.

The loin chop comes from the center and rear section of the loin. The bone will be the shape of a T, much like a porterhouse steak. One side of the bone will have the firm loin muscle similar to a New York strip steak. The other side may or may not have the tenderloin attached. Some folks like the tenderloin attached and others prefer not to have it. You may see the loin chops with a large tenderloin portion sold as tenderloin chops. When choosing a loin chop, look for the ones that you prefer. The loin chop is best cut ¾ to 1½ inches thick.

The sirloin chop comes from the rear of the loin. It's similar to a top sirloin steak, including being on the chewier side. The color is a little darker than that of the loin and rib chops, and the meat is a bit bolder. Sirloin chops are typically a little less expensive than the others and can be substituted as you wish. These are available bone-in or boneless, though each requires the same amount of time to cook. The sirloin chop is best cut ¾ to 1 inch thick.

The boneless pork tenderloin chop is simply a thick slice of boneless pork tenderloin. It's the filet mignon of pork and has a similar texture. If cutting them yourself, be sure to remove the silver skin from the whole tenderloin before cutting it into chops. These are very lean and should be cooked quickly, taking care not to overcook. Boneless pork tenderloin chops are best cut 1 to 1½ inches thick.

Lamb chops are typically available bone-in as rib chops and loin chops. The rib chops are tender and juicy and are often served with the bones frenched. These are sometimes called "lamb lollipops" because of their appearance. Lamb rib chops are best cut ¾ to 1¼ inches thick. Lamb loin chops look like little T-bone steaks. The meat is firm and tasty and best cooked to your desired degree of doneness like a steak. Lamb loin chops are best cut 1¼ to 2 inches thick.

Veal chops, same as lamb chops, are available bone-in as rib chops and loin chops. The veal rib chop often has the bone frenched and the veal loin chop looks like a small porterhouse. You'll notice the pinkish color of a veal chop that makes it look similar to pork, but it's actually young beef. Much like a steak, both cuts of veal chops should be served cooked to your desired degree of doneness. Feel free to substitute one for the other in a recipe. Veal chops are best cut 1 to 1½ inches thick.

GRADING CHOPS

Pork doesn't get graded for quality by the USDA because, unlike beef, it's very consistent. The meat will all have similar marbling. Be sure to pay attention at the meat case, though, because sometimes you'll find great cuts of pork that would be graded "prime" if the USDA did grade pork by quality—a lot of marbling is always a good thing for the cook. There is one other option to consider when choosing pork. There are heritage breeds that have become very popular among small farmers and chefs. Berkshire and Duroc are the two most common heritage breeds that you'll find. This pork shows up in some high-end markets and at farmers' markets around the country. If it's available, you might want to give it a try. It's a little different from what's in the stores these days, but it's very tasty and you may like it.

Lamb and veal do get graded for quality by the USDA, and the grades are similar to those for beef (see page 80). It's unlikely that you'll see choices, but if you do, choose the USDA Choice or Prime if either is available. Lamb should also be labeled as imported or American grown. I prefer the American lamb.

GRILLING THE CHOPS

There are many ways to cook a chop, but by far the favorite of most people is on the grill. When properly grilled, the chops will have a little bit of char on the outside and be tender and juicy on the inside. A bit of smoky flavor from the grill is a great addition to the taste of a chop. I've even added a bunch of fresh herbs to the fire on occasion to enhance the flavor of my chops. Those beautiful crosshatch grill marks enhance the look of chops, so be sure to lay the chops on the cooking grate in a way that will have the marks going on an angle across the chop. After about 3 minutes, rotate the chop 90 degrees and cook for another 2 to 3 minutes to complete the look. Then, flip the chop and cook to your desired degree of doneness. I've given you some tasty recipes in this chapter, but, by all means, feel free to mix and match parts of them to your liking, or combine part of one of my recipes with an old favorite grilling recipe of your own.

COOKING TIMES FOR PORK CHOPS

These times and temperatures are for 1-inch-thick pork chops cooked on a hot direct barbecue grill. Most people don't want their pork served too rare, even though it's safe. Remember that temperatures vary slightly from grill to grill, so your times may differ a little from the following times. If you're not sure, just cut into one of the chops. It's better to serve a chop with a cut in it than one that's overcooked.

A little bit pink-tender and juicy: 4 to 5 minutes per side*

Done the way your grandma did it—Gray and dry: 6 to 8 minutes per side*

Let rest for 5 minutes before serving.

COOKING TIMES FOR LAMB CHOPS

For lamb loin chops 1½ inches thick, grill over direct high heat. If you're not sure, just cut into one of the chops. It's better to serve a chop with a cut in it than one that's overcooked.

Medium-rare, pink-tender, and juicy: 4 to 5 minutes per side*
Medium-well, gray, and beginning to dry: 6 to 7 minutes per side*

Let rest for 5 minutes before serving.

COOKING TIMES FOR VEAL CHOPS

For veal loin or rib chops 1¼ inches thick, grill over direct high heat. If you're not sure, just cut into one of the chops. It's better to serve a chop with a cut in it than one that's overcooked.

Medium-rare, pink-tender, and juicy: 4 to 5 minutes per side*
Medium-well, gray, and beginning to dry: 6 to 7 minutes per side*

Let rest for 5 minutes before serving.

SEASONING THE CHOPS

Much like a steak, once you've picked your chops and come up with a cooking plan, you'll need to season them to enhance their great flavor. Salt and pepper surely works well and I use them often. You might also try the Steak Seasoning Salt (page 82) or the Big Bold Steak Spice (page 82) recipes from the steak chapter. None of the seasonings in this book are specific to the cut or choice of meat, but I often like to add some herbs to my pork, so I've given you a recipe here for Tasty Pork Chop Seasoning. I've also used a simple brine for the Sweet Maple–Brined Pork Chops (page 72), and that can be used with any type of chop. Just be careful not to combine the brine and a rub because the end result will be too salty. Chops can be paired nicely with sweet or savory toppings, too. I've done a nice grilled Vidalia onion topping for the pork-chop sandwiches and a barbecue version of the classic Oscar topping for the veal chops. Mix, match, and enjoy.

TASTY PORK CHOP SEASONING
MAKES ABOUT ⅜ CUP

3 tablespoons salt

1 tablespoon finely ground black pepper

½ tablespoon granulated garlic

½ tablespoon onion powder

½ tablespoon paprika

½ tablespoon lemon pepper

½ teaspoon dried tarragon leaves

½ teaspoon dried thyme leaves

½ teaspoon Sugar In The Raw

Mix together and keep in an airtight container.

PORK CHOP SANDWICH WITH GRILLED VIDALIA ONIONS

6
SERVINGS

In Chicago, neighborhood hot-dog stands serve a pork chop sandwich that's a little different than expected. First off, it's served on a bun, but the pork chop has a bone in it. Seems crazy but that's the tradition and everyone knows to eat around the bone as you go. The other unique thing about that sandwich is the grilled onions. They start out with a huge pile of sliced onions on the flat-top grill and cook them down until they are brown and crunchy and loaded with flavor. My sandwich is a little more civilized because we use boneless pork chops and sweet and delicious Vidalia onions. Be sure to cook them until they are all brown and crunchy, and put plenty on your sandwich. These would go very well served with home fries and coleslaw.

2 tablespoons olive oil

1 large Vidalia onion, thinly sliced and rings separated

2 tablespoons balsamic vinegar

2 tablespoons soy sauce

1 teaspoon brown sugar

½ teaspoon black pepper

. . . . .

6 boneless pork chops, ½ inch thick

Tasty Pork Chop Seasoning (page 53), as needed

6 kaiser rolls, split

❶ In a large skillet over medium heat, heat the oil. Add the onion and cook for 7 to 8 minutes, stirring occasionally, until the onion begins to soften and turn brown. Add the vinegar, soy sauce, brown sugar, and pepper and mix well. Cook for another 7 to 8 minutes, until the onion is deep brown and very soft. Transfer to a bowl and set aside. ❷ Season the chops liberally on both sides with the Tasty Pork Chop Seasoning. ❸ Prepare the grill for cooking over direct high heat. Quickly toast the buns on the cooking grate and remove to a platter. Place the chops directly on the cooking grate and cook for 3 minutes. Flip and top with the onion mixture, dividing it evenly among them. Cook for another 3 minutes and remove chops to the buns.

PORK TENDERLOIN MEDALLION CHOPS WRAPPED IN BACON WITH AN APPLE GLAZE

SERVINGS

Everything goes better with bacon! These little pork tenderloin chops are really the filet mignon of pork, so I like the idea of wrapping them in bacon just like you would a steak. They're quite a bit smaller, though, so you'll want to allow for 2 to 3 per guest like I have here. Be sure to use thinly sliced bacon so it will get cooked through at the same time as the tenderloin chop. It's okay to overlap it a little and secure it with a wooden toothpick or a skewer. Be sure to retrieve all the toothpicks before you serve them to your guests so they won't have to go looking. The apple glaze is very simple but makes a perfect accompaniment to the pork and bacon combo. These would go very well served with a rice pilaf and green peas.

GLAZE
3 cups apple juice

1 tablespoon Sugar In The Raw

• • • • •

12 slices thinly sliced bacon

12 pork tenderloin medallion chops, about 1½ inches thick

Black pepper

❶ Soak 12 toothpicks in water for at least 1 hour.
❷ To make the glaze: In a medium saucepan over medium-high heat, heat the apple juice. Bring to a slow boil and cook for 15 to 20 minutes, until reduced to 1 cup. Add the sugar and mix well. Transfer to a bowl and set aside to cool. ❸ Wrap a slice of bacon around the circumference of each tenderloin medallion and secure with a toothpick. Season each chop lightly on both sides with black pepper. ❹ Prepare the grill for cooking over direct medium heat. Place the chops directly on the cooking grate. Cook for 3 minutes. Flip and cook for 3 more minutes. Flip and brush with the prepared glaze. Cook for 1 minute. Brush again, flip, and brush the other side. Cook for 1 more minute and brush again. Flip and brush two more times cooking for 1 minute each time. Remove to a platter and let rest for 3 minutes before serving.

BOURBON-SOAKED PORK CHOPS

6 SERVINGS

Pork chops do very well when you marinate them before grilling. The subtle white meat of the pork picks up the flavors of a marinade in a short amount of time and carries them well. The marinade also helps keep the chops juicy during the cooking. A simple marinade of Italian dressing can work wonderfully on pork, but stronger marinades can really make for an exciting dinner. For this recipe, I've used Kentucky bourbon. It matches beautifully with the grilled chops and gives them an exotic flavor when paired with the Dijon mustard and the other common marinade ingredients. A marinade is all about balance and this one is just right with the boneless loin chops. These would go very well served with glazed carrots and cornbread.

MARINADE
½ cup Kentucky bourbon
(I like Woodford Reserve)

¼ cup Dijon mustard

2 tablespoons soy sauce

2 tablespoons honey

1 teaspoon onion powder

¼ teaspoon cayenne pepper

2 cloves garlic, crushed

• • • • •

6 boneless pork loin chops, about 1½ inches thick

❶ To make the marinade: In a small bowl, whisk together the bourbon, mustard, soy sauce, honey, onion powder, cayenne, and garlic. Set aside. Place the six chops in a glass dish and pour the marinade over them. Turn to coat. Cover and refrigerate for at least 4 hours and up to 12 hours, turning the chops to coat every 2 hours. ❷ Prepare the grill for cooking over direct high heat. Remove the chops from the marinade and place directly on the cooking grate. Cook for 4 minutes. Flip and cook for another 4 to 5 minutes for slightly pink and juicy, or to your desired degree of doneness. Remove to a platter and let rest for 4 minutes before serving.

PORK CHOPS WITH PEACH SALSA

SERVINGS

Pork chops are a wonderful canvas for the cook to work with. They go well with so many different flavors. Fruits are a great match with any pork, and a little spice goes well with it, too. The sweet and spicy flavor of peach salsa is a perfect pairing with grilled pork chops. I like to use canned tomatoes, for their consistency, and fresh peaches when I make salsa, but canned peaches can be drained to substitute in a pinch. This Peach Salsa goes well with chips or as a topping for nachos. For this recipe, I've chosen boneless loin chops but you can use the bone-in variety as well. These would go very well served with a crispy slaw and a sweet potato casserole.

PEACH SALSA

1½ cups finely diced peaches (about 2 medium peaches)

½ medium red onion, finely chopped

½ large green bell pepper, finely chopped

½ cup thinly sliced scallions, white and green parts

1 jalapeño, seeded and finely chopped (leave the seeds in if you like more heat)

2 cloves garlic, crushed

One 10-ounce can diced tomatoes with green chiles, drained

Juice of ½ lime

½ teaspoon salt

½ teaspoon finely ground black pepper

• • • • •

6 boneless pork loin chops, 1¼ inches thick

Tasty Pork Chop Seasoning (page 53), as needed

❶ To make the salsa: Put the peaches, onion, bell pepper, scallions, jalapeño, and garlic in a large bowl. Mix well. Add the tomatoes and mix again. Add the lime juice, salt, and pepper and mix again. Refrigerate for 30 minutes. Mix again and check that the salt seasoning is adequate. Cover and set aside at room temperature. ❷ Season the chops liberally on both sides with the Tasty Pork Chop Seasoning. ❸ Prepare the grill for cooking over direct medium-high heat. Place the pork chops directly on the cooking grate. Cook for 5 minutes. Flip and cook for another 4 minutes for slightly pink and juicy, or to your desired degree of doneness. Remove to a platter and let rest for 4 minutes. To serve, top each chop with ½ cup of the salsa.

GRILLED STUFFED PORK CHOPS WITH DRIED CHERRIES AND BACON

6

SERVINGS

I love to stuff pork chops, but there are a few rules you need to follow when stuffing them. First is to get thick pork chops. You'll need them at least 1½ inches thick, though 2 inches thick is preferable, so that after you stuff them, there is enough meat on both sides to allow you to cook the chops long enough to get the outside nicely browned. Next, you'll need to cut a pocket into each chop, or have the meat man at the store do it for you. The pocket needs to be as deep as possible while the opening stays as small as possible to keep the stuffing in while it's cooking. Last but not least, the stuffing should be made up only of fully cooked ingredients. Even a thick chop won't be able to cook long enough to get a stuffing with raw ingredients cooked without drying out the chop. So, I like to sauté the ingredients ahead of time and cook any meat that I may use, like bacon or sausage, all the way through. This way, while the chop cooks, the stuffing heats up perfectly, and it can all be eaten while tender and juicy. I'd also recommend using only a small amount of stuffing in each chop. That's why I like to use intensely flavored ingredients, like dried fruit and bacon. These would go very well served with baked sweet potatoes and green beans.

continued on next page . . .

. . . continued

STUFFING
2 cups packaged cornbread stuffing

1 tablespoon olive oil

¼ cup finely chopped celery

¼ cup finely chopped onion

3 slices bacon, cooked and crumbled

¼ cup dried cherries, finely chopped

½ cup vegetable stock

2 tablespoons real maple syrup

Pinch of cayenne pepper

Pinch of salt

• • • • •

6 boneless pork loin chops, 2 inches thick, with deep pockets cut in the side for stuffing

Tasty Pork Chop Seasoning (page 53), as needed

❶ To make the stuffing: Place the cornbread stuffing in a large bowl. In a small nonstick skillet over medium heat, heat the oil. Add the celery and onion and cook for 3 to 4 minutes, stirring often, until soft. Add to the cornbread and mix well. Add the bacon, cherries, stock, maple syrup, cayenne, and salt. Mix well. Let rest for 5 minutes and mix again. ❷ Prepare the grill for cooking over direct medium-high heat. Divide the stuffing equally among the chops' pockets, pushing into the pocket as deeply as possible. Squeeze the opening of the pocket shut to seal it. Season the chops liberally on both sides with the Tasty Pork Chop Seasoning. Place the chops directly on the cooking grate. Cook for 5 minutes. Flip and cook for another 5 minutes for slightly pink and juicy chops, or to your desired degree of doneness. Remove to a platter and let rest for 5 minutes before serving.

EXTRA-THICK PORK CHOPS WITH HOMEMADE BARBECUE SAUCE

SERVINGS

This is a classic way to serve grilled pork chops and a favorite of many. It's simply a typical barbecue rub for seasoning and a glaze of barbecue sauce to finish. The exciting part of this recipe is the homemade barbecue sauce. There are many good sauces available in stores and online, but sometimes it's fun to make it from scratch. This is a pretty middle-of-the-road barbecue sauce recipe. Feel free to doctor it to your liking with a little extra heat, or a little extra sweet, or whatever your favorite addition may be. In many of the recipes in this book, I call for your favorite barbecue sauce. Well, this just might be your new favorite barbecue sauce, so feel free to use it in all of those places. Of course, your favorite might come from a bottle or may be an old family recipe, so go ahead and substitute yours in this recipe as well. These would go very well served with potato salad and baked beans.

HOMEMADE BARBECUE SAUCE

2 tablespoons butter

½ cup finely chopped onion

2 cloves garlic, crushed

¾ cup ketchup

¾ cup prepared chili sauce

¼ cup apple cider vinegar

2 tablespoons yellow mustard

1 tablespoon soy sauce

1 tablespoon Worcestershire sauce

1 tablespoon Louisiana hot sauce

Juice of ½ lemon

½ teaspoon black pepper

½ cup brown sugar

. . . . .

6 center-cut pork loin T-bone chops, 1½ inches thick

Tasty Pork Chop Seasoning (page 53), as needed

1 To make the barbecue sauce: In a medium sauce-pan over medium heat, melt the butter. Add the onion and garlic and cook for about 4 minutes, stirring often, until the onion is very soft. Add the ketchup, chili sauce, vinegar, mustard, soy sauce, Worcestershire sauce, hot sauce, lemon juice, and pepper. Mix well and bring to a simmer. Reduce the heat to low and add the brown sugar. Mix well and cook for 5 minutes, stirring often. Remove from the heat. Divide the sauce equally between two bowls, one for brushing on the chops as they grill

continued on next page . . .

. . . continued

and one for serving at the table. ❷ Season the chops liberally on both sides with the Tasty Pork Chop Seasoning. ❸ Prepare the grill for cooking over direct medium-high heat. Place the chops directly on the cooking grate. Cook for 3 minutes. Flip and cook for another 3 minutes. Brush with sauce and continue cooking, flipping, and brushing with sauce for another 6 minutes total for slightly pink and juicy, or to your desired degree of doneness. Discard the sauce that you've been brushing with. Remove the chops to a platter and serve with the second bowl of sauce on the side.

COFFEE-RUBBED PORK CHOPS

6

I make a lot of different rubs for grilling. I use a lot of interesting ingredients in them, but one of my favorites is ground coffee. I use regular ol' ground coffee, preferably finely ground. While you might think the grounds would be grainy and strong, you'll be pleasantly surprised to learn that they melt in just like all the other spices. The earthy flavor is like nothing else and it blends beautifully with garlic, onion, chili powder, and all the other staples of a good barbecue rub. When cooked on the chops, the grounds add a deep flavor hinting of coffee without overpowering the other ingredients in the rub. I've made a simple rub here, but go ahead and add a few things if you're feeling adventurous. And if you're in the mood for a sauce with the chops, try mixing a little brewed coffee in with your favorite barbecue sauce and brushing it on during the last couple of minutes of grilling. These would go very well served with a baked potato and steamed cauliflower.

COFFEE RUB

1 tablespoon salt

1 teaspoon finely ground coffee

1 teaspoon paprika

½ teaspoon granulated garlic

½ teaspoon lemon pepper

· · · · ·

6 center-cut, bone-in pork loin chops, 1¼ inches thick

❶ To make the rub: Combine the salt, coffee, paprika, granulated garlic, and lemon pepper in a small bowl. Mix well. **❷** Season the pork chops evenly on both sides with the rub. **❸** Prepare the grill for cooking over direct medium-high heat. Place the chops directly on the cooking grate. Cook for 5 minutes. Flip and cook for another 5 minutes for slightly pink and juicy, or to your desired degree of doneness. Remove to a platter and let rest for 4 minutes before serving.

MARSHA'S SMOTHERED PORK CHOPS

This recipe comes from my good friend Marsha Russell of Lynchburg, Tennessee. She cooks good food that I like to eat, so I always put one of her recipes in my books. This one is a keeper. The chops are tasty and tender and the vegetables help make an amazing sauce. These would go very well served with white rice and homemade biscuits.

1 cup plus 2 tablespoons flour

1½ teaspoons salt

1½ teaspoons finely ground black pepper

¼ cup oil

6 bone-in pork loin chops, 1 inch thick

1 medium onion, chopped

1 large green bell pepper, chopped

2 stalks celery, chopped

2 cloves garlic, chopped

1 jalapeño, finely chopped

One 14.5-ounce can vegetable broth

1 teaspoon gravy base browning sauce (I use Gravy Master)

❶ Preheat the oven to 350 degrees F. In a deep pie dish, mix together the 1 cup of flour, 1 teaspoon of the salt, and 1 teaspoon of the pepper. In a large skillet over medium high heat, heat the oil. Dredge three of the pork chops in the flour mixture, coating them well, then put them in the skillet. ❷ Cook the chops for about 4 minutes, until golden brown. Flip and cook for another 4 minutes, until golden brown. Transfer the browned chops to a 9-x-13-inch baking pan. Repeat dredging and browning the remaining 3 chops. Transfer the second batch of chops to the baking pan. Reserve the oil. Add the onion, bell pepper, celery, garlic, and jalapeño to the skillet with the reserved oil. Cook for about 4 minutes, stirring often, until the onion is soft. Sprinkle the remaining 2 tablespoons flour over the vegetables and mix well. Continue cooking, stirring often, for 1 minute. Add the vegetable broth, the remaining

½ teaspoon salt and ½ teaspoon pepper, and the gravy base. Mix well and bring to a simmer, stirring often. Pour the vegetable mixture evenly over the pork chops. ❸ Cover tightly with foil and bake for 1 hour. Remove from the oven and let rest for 10 minutes. To serve, place a pork chop on each plate and spoon the vegetable mixture over the top. Use the vegetable mixture as a gravy for rice, mashed potatoes, or noodles.

SWEET MAPLE-BRINED PORK CHOPS

4
SERVINGS

Brining is the process whereby meat is submerged in a solution with a salt content higher than its own. This creates a transfer of the brine into the meat, which makes it juicier when cooked. The good news is the brine will also carry any flavors that you add to it. For this recipe, that flavor is maple syrup and it goes very nicely with the taste of the juicy brined pork rib chops. When brining small cuts of meat like these chops, or pieces of chicken, you have to be careful not to have the brine be too salty and you can't let the chops soak for too long. Otherwise, the chops will get too salty and take on a firm texture similar to that of cured ham. For the brine I've used here, three hours works well. If you like the brine taste to be a little stronger, try brining for four or five hours, but I wouldn't recommend longer than that. These would go very well served with potato pancakes and apple sauce.

BRINE

1 cup water

¼ cup real maple syrup

2 tablespoons kosher salt

1 teaspoon lemon pepper

1 cup ice water

· · · · ·

4 center-cut pork rib chops, about 1¼ inches thick

Maple syrup, as needed

❶ To make the brine: In a small saucepan over medium-high heat, heat the water for 2 minutes. Add the syrup, salt, and lemon pepper and mix well. As soon as the salt dissolves, remove from the heat. Transfer to a bowl and add the ice water. Stir well and refrigerate until cold.

❷ Put the chops in a gallon-size zip-top bag. Pour the brine over them. Remove as much air as possible and seal the bag. Place in a bowl and refrigerate for 3 hours, turning occasionally. Remove the chops from the brine and rinse well with tap water. Dry each chop well and transfer to a plate. ❸ Prepare the grill for cooking over direct high heat. Place the chops directly on the cooking grate. Cook for 4 minutes. Flip and cook for 3 to 4 minutes for slightly pink and juicy chops, or to your desired degree of doneness. Remove to a platter and let rest for 5 minutes. Drizzle with a little bit of maple syrup before serving.

GRILLED VEAL CHOPS OSCAR

4 SERVINGS

Veal Oscar was named in honor of King Oscar II (1829–1907), king of Sweden and Norway, because this is how he liked his veal. Since then, a lot of other people have liked theirs served this way as well. The traditional version uses thinly sliced veal cutlets sautéed in a pan. The cutlets are then topped with crabmeat, asparagus, and a béarnaise sauce. For the grill, we're using a veal chop, and instead of the béarnaise, we're going to top it with a slice of Jack cheese. It's not quite as elegant as the béarnaise, but it's creamy and delicious and brings the flavors together nicely. You can substitute a béarnaise sauce, if you'd like. These would go very well served with a rice pilaf.

8 spears asparagus

1 cup Italian dressing

4 veal rib chops, 1¼ inches thick

Tasty Pork Chop Seasoning (page 53), as needed

4 slices Monterey Jack cheese

1 cup cooked lump crabmeat

❶ Put the asparagus in a glass dish and pour the Italian dressing over it. Toss well to coat and set aside. ❷ Season the chops liberally on both sides with the Tasty Pork Chop Seasoning. Refrigerate. ❸ Prepare the grill for cooking over direct medium-high heat. Remove the asparagus from the dressing and put it directly on the cooking grate. Cook for 2 minutes. Place the chops directly on the cooking grate. Cook for 4 minutes. Flip the chops, and top each one with a slice of cheese, ¼ cup of the crabmeat, and two of the asparagus spears. Close the lid and cook for another 3 to 4 minutes for medium-rare, or to your desired degree of doneness. Transfer to a platter and let rest for 5 minutes before serving.

DOUBLE-THICK LAMB CHOPS WITH BALSAMIC-HONEY GLAZE

4
SERVINGS

In this recipe I call for double-thick lamb loin chops, but you can substitute lamb rib chops. I'd also suggest using thinner chops if you like them well-done because the thick ones lend themselves much better to serving medium-rare or even rare. You could even substitute a rack of lamb for the chops—it's really the same thing, only it's not cut up. Just be sure to add a little extra cooking time if you do. The glaze can be adjusted as you like, but you'd do best to stay with the balsamic vinegar for a base. A little more honey would sweeten it up and you could substitute ¼ cup raspberry or peach preserves for the honey if you'd like to add a fruity twist to the taste. These would go very well served with couscous and grilled squash.

BALSAMIC-HONEY GLAZE

2 cups balsamic vinegar

2 cloves garlic

1 bay leaf

1 teaspoon honey

• • • • •

2 teaspoons salt

1 teaspoon black pepper

1 teaspoon granulated garlic

8 lamb loin chops, 1¼ inches thick

❶ To make the glaze: In a medium saucepan over medium heat, combine the balsamic vinegar, garlic cloves, and bay leaf. Bring to a simmer and cook for about 20 minutes, until reduced to about ¾ cup. Remove, discard the garlic and bay leaf, and stir in the honey. Transfer to a bowl and set aside. ❷ Combine the salt, pepper, and granulated garlic in a small bowl. Season the chops liberally on both sides with the salt mixture. ❸ Prepare the grill for cooking over direct medium-high heat. Place the lamb chops directly on the cooking grate. Cook for 4 minutes. Flip and cook for 3 to 4 more minutes for medium-rare, or to your desired degree of doneness. Remove to a platter and let rest for 3 minutes. To serve, drizzle 4 dinner plates with a small amount of the balsamic glaze and top each with 2 lamb chops. Serve the remaining glaze on the side.

I LOVE STEAK. WHO DOESN'T? IT'S THE ABSOLUTE FAVORITE FOOD OF MOST AMERICANS. WHEN WE HAVE REASON TO CELEBRATE, MOST OF

us do it with big, juicy, tender steaks. When a big business deal needs to be discussed over dinner, it will usually be at a steakhouse. On my birthday, when it's my choice, we're having steak for dinner. We do all differ on our favorite cut of steak, though. I'm a sirloin guy with rib-eye as my backup, but I know many of you will stand by the filet mignon as the best. And let's not forget the New York strip steak, which has a loyal following of its own and may just be the best when dry aged. But the king of all steaks is a big porterhouse, which includes a strip and a filet, cooked on the bone. And who doesn't like that? There are a few things you need to know when buying steaks.

Chapter 3: **STEAKS**

STEAKS RECIPES

STEAK CHOICES

First, you'll have to choose the cut of steak that you're going to serve. Many different cuts of meat are called *steaks* these days, but for this book we're only going to discuss the cuts that can be broiled or grilled and served rare to medium-well for a tender, juicy steak dinner. The most popular of the true steaks are all cut from high on the cow in the loin area. These include the porterhouse, T-bone, filet mignon, New York strip, rib eye, and the top sirloin. When you visit a high-end steakhouse, these are the cuts you'll see. And they are the best of the best. A newcomer to the lineup of tender steaks is the flat-iron steak. It's actually cut from the chuck, generally a tough part of the cow, but because it's a muscle that just doesn't get much use, it remains tender. So tender, in fact, that it's considered to be second only to the filet mignon in the tenderness department, with a great taste similar to that of top sirloin. A general rule of thumb when it comes to steaks is that the most tender cuts don't have the most flavor and the tastiest cuts have a little more of a chew to them. It's a kind of yin and yang, but most of us can easily find the combination and cut of steak that suit us best.

CUTS OF STEAK

The porterhouse is a big steak cut from the rear section of the loin, also known as the short loin, and is always served on the bone. It consists of a large portion of filet mignon and an even larger portion of New York strip. This is a man-sized steak and should be cut at least 1¼ inches thick, but is often cut 2 inches thick, or more, and served as a steak for two.

The T-bone is the little brother of the porterhouse and is aptly named after the shape of its bone. It's cut from the middle section of the short loin, and it, too, is always served on the bone. The main difference between the T-bone and the porterhouse is the size of the filet. It will be considerably smaller on the T-bone, which makes this a better choice for those who aren't quite up to a big porterhouse. The T-bone should be cut to a minimum of 1¼ inches thick.

The filet mignon is often called the queen of steaks. The tenderness is second to none and a filet of good quality can truly be cut with just a fork. Filet mignon is cut from the tenderloin muscle of the short loin and is always served boneless. The filet is a favorite among light eaters because it is a small steak by nature and can be cut thick without producing a huge steak. A filet is best cut at least 1½ inches thick.

New York strip steak is cut from the boneless strip loin muscle and is well known for its deep flavor and great texture. It's not the melt-in-your-mouth texture of a filet mignon, but more of an enjoyable chew, and many consider the taste-to-tenderness ratio of this steak to be the best. It's also considered to be the best candidate for true dry aging. The New York strip steak should be cut to a minimum of 1¼ inches thick.

The rib eye is cut from the rib section, which is the front of the loin. It's the most heavily marbled of the steak cuts and is revered for the flavor that comes with the marbling. It can be served on or off the bone without much difference. The rib-eye steak is the same part of the cow that gives us the standing rib roast, or prime rib. While technically not a steak when cooked as a roast, it's the same piece of meat and loved by many a carnivore. The rib-eye steak should be cut to a minimum of 1¼ inches thick.

The top sirloin steak is cut from the rear of the loin. It's generally considered to be the most flavorful of the steak cuts, while not necessarily the most tender. It's a big steak, well suited for two or more when cooked whole. It's best when cut at least 1 inch thick and preferably thicker. A 2-inch-thick top sirloin can be cooked like a steak, then sliced and served to multiple guests much like a roast.

The flank steak is cut from the lower part of the cow and has a very distinctive grain and flavor. It's also the only steak that is cooked as one whole muscle without being cut. For that reason there is no recommendation for thickness. These are typically about 1¼ inches thick and that's fine. The texture is dense with virtually no marbling and no fat on the outside. If cooked properly to a rare or medium-rare degree of doneness, it can be tender and juicy, but if cooked beyond medium-rare, it will quickly get tough and dry. If your guests don't care for rare meat, a flank steak probably isn't the best

choice that day. The flank steak has a rich beefy flavor that takes very well to interesting marinades. I like to use Asian flavors, citrus, lots of garlic, and, sometimes, fresh herbs to marinate my flank steaks. When slicing a flank steak, be sure to cut thin slices across the grain.

The flat-iron steak is a fairly new cut. It's actually a muscle within the chuck that was always just part of a big chuck roast until someone figured out that there was a gem in there. The flat iron isn't the prettiest steak and the sizes are a little bit random but the price is usually a bargain, and I consider it to be one of the best steaks there is. They're readily available in supermarkets and if you don't see them just ask the meat man. If you haven't tried one of these, you really should.

The round steak comes from high on the rear leg of the cow, and it's not a tender cut like the others I've listed. But it does have a very good beef flavor, so if you start with one that's only ½ inch thick, pound it, and marinate it, you'll be able to grill it and have a steak that's tender enough to enjoy. But here I've used it in my alternative-to-the-grill recipe, Mrs. Rice's Pepper Steak. It's perfectly suited for a slow-cooked dish like that.

The skirt steak is quite unique in its appearance, texture, and taste. The steak is only a few inches wide, less than an inch thick, and a couple of feet long. The grain is very distinct and runs directly across the short width. Skirt steak is best cut into pieces that are 5 to 6 inches long, so they can be easily carved across the grain after cooking. Skirt steak can be served in portions like a typical steak, but is often served sliced as the main ingredient in fajitas.

The pork steak as you suspect is pork instead of beef. It's actually a slice of the pork butt and it's delicious when grilled. Like many cities, St. Louis has its own signature dish and theirs is the pork steak. They typically grill it for a while, and then finish it in a pan with barbecue sauce. I've included that recipe, but remember, pork steaks are also good just grilled, like a tender steak. For St. Louis–style cooking, I like them between ¾ and 1 inch thick, but for grilling ¾ inch is the right thickness.

The tuna steak is, of course, tuna. If you're not used to eating fresh tuna you are in for a real treat. It's really more like cooking a piece of meat than it is fish. It's red and has beautiful texture, and does well with a charred outside and a very rare inside. It's best cut at least 1¼ inches thick and comes in many varieties. Superfresh ahi is my favorite.

GRADING STEAKS

The USDA grades beef for us and there are three grades that you will find at the market. The biggest difference between the three grades is how much marbling they have. Marbling is the lines of fat within the muscle of the steak, and the more, the better because marbling is what makes a steak tender and juicy. Clearly these are two very important things when it comes to steak.

* USDA Prime is the highest grade of beef with amazing tenderness, juiciness, and flavor. It has the highest degree of marbling and is usually derived from younger beef. USDA Prime steaks are served at the most exclusive upscale steakhouses. It's rarely available at the supermarket, so look for an upscale butcher or order your USDA Prime steaks online. An excellent source is www.allenbrothers.com.

* USDA Choice is the middle grade of beef and the most common in supermarkets and restaurants. It has less marbling than the Prime meat but is usually good enough for a tasty and tender steak as long as you stay with the tender cuts. Choice meat will also be considerably cheaper than Prime, so it is the choice of most steak buyers.

* USDA Select is the poorest of the three most common grades. This is generally the lowest grade of steak you will find at a supermarket or restaurant. It has very little marbling and therefore it's tougher, leaner, and less flavorful and subsequently, less enjoyable than the other two grades.

GRILLING THE STEAKS

Most of the recipes here are geared for outdoor grilling. But they can all be easily done on an indoor grill or in the broiler. You may have to adjust the cooking times a bit to fit your equipment. I've suggested thicknesses for the specific steaks both here and in the recipes. In general, thicker steaks will cook better. If a steak is too thin, it will be cooked before the outside gets a chance to get nice and crusty, and that crust makes for a great-tasting steak. A hot fire will help with this as well, but all grills are different and your times, temps, and crustiness will vary. To encourage the great caramelization and appearance of your steak, you might want to use a cast-iron cooking grate. Many grills offer cast-iron grates as an option and some even have them as a standard feature. If yours doesn't, you should be able to find a small cast-iron searing grate that will fit on top of the regular grate of most grills. To use the cast-iron grate properly, make sure to heat it thoroughly on the grill. Then, place the steaks on it and cook for 3 minutes. Rotate the steak (don't flip) 90 degrees and cook for another 3 minutes. This will give you those beautiful crosshatch marks. Now flip the steak and cook to your desired degree of doneness. Just be sure to serve it with the beautifully marked side facing up.

COOKING TIMES FOR STEAKS

These are general guidelines for steaks that are 1¼ inches thick, cooked on a hot direct barbecue grill. I've also included a description of the common degrees of doneness for steaks. Remember that temperatures vary slightly from grill to grill, so your times may differ a little from the following times. If you're not sure, just cut into one of the steaks. It's better to serve a steak with a cut in it than one that's overcooked.

RARE
Red inside with a cool center: 2 to 3 minutes per side*
Approximate internal temperature: 120 degrees F

MEDIUM-RARE
Pink inside but juicy and tender: 3 to 4 minutes per side*
Approximate internal temperature: 130 degrees F

MEDIUM
Pink fading to gray inside: 4 to 5 minutes per side*
Approximate internal temperature: 140 degrees F

MEDIUM-WELL
Gray inside and beginning to toughen up:
5 to 6 minutes per side*
Approximate internal temperature: 150 degrees F

WELL-DONE
Gray inside, dry, and chewy: 6 to 7 minutes per side*
Approximate internal temperature: 160 degrees F

Let rest for 5 minutes before serving.

SEASONING THE STEAKS

Once you've chosen your steak and have a plan to get it done properly, you'll need to consider the seasoning that you'll be using to enhance the flavor. While some steak lovers prefer plain old salt and pepper, others like to add a few more traditional flavors like garlic and onion. Still others prefer to really spice things up with a complex blend of spices that brings out the flavors of the steak in a big way. These all seem like good ideas to me. It just depends on the mood I'm in that day. I've included two steak seasoning blends for you to use in the recipes that follow. One is a simple Steak Seasoning Salt and the other is a more intense option we'll call Big Bold Steak Spice. Feel free to substitute one for the other in the recipes, based on your preference and mood. Steaks can be topped as well, classically with blue cheese, grilled onions, sautéed mushrooms, flavored butters, or béarnaise sauce. I've added some of these in the recipes here, but feel free to mix and match them as you like.

STEAK SEASONING SALT

MAKES ⅜ CUP

3 tablespoons salt

1 tablespoon granulated garlic

1 tablespoon onion powder

1 tablespoon finely ground black pepper

Mix together and keep in an airtight container.

BIG BOLD STEAK SPICE

MAKES ABOUT ½ CUP

3 tablespoons salt

1 tablespoon onion powder

1 tablespoon finely ground black pepper

1 teaspoon smoked paprika

1 teaspoon ground coriander

1 teaspoon good-quality chili powder

1 teaspoon Sugar In The Raw

½ teaspoon dry mustard

Mix together and keep in an airtight container.

KING OF STEAKS: THE PORTERHOUSE WITH A HOMEMADE STEAK SAUCE

4

SERVINGS

I consider the porterhouse to be the king of steaks. It's a big manly steak that's always cooked on the bone. Cooking a steak on the bone not only gives it big flavor but a great look as well. And, of course, the bone makes for a nice doggy bag. On one side of the porterhouse is the wonderful full-bodied taste of a New York strip steak and on the other side is the luxurious tenderness of a filet mignon—the best of both worlds. The steak sauce in this recipe is a great match for the porterhouse, but can also go well with any other cut of steak. These would go very well served with a baked potato and creamed corn.

4 porterhouse steaks, about 1¼ inches thick

Big Bold Steak Spice (facing page), as needed

• • • • •

HOMEMADE STEAK SAUCE

2 cups low-sodium beef broth

2 tablespoons butter

2 tablespoons finely chopped onion

1 clove garlic, crushed

2 teaspoons flour

1½ teaspoons prepared horseradish

1 teaspoon prepared chili sauce

½ teaspoon black pepper

❶ Season the steaks liberally on both sides with the Big Bold Steak Spice. Refrigerate. ❷ To make the sauce: Pour the beef broth into a medium saucepan over medium heat and cook for about 15 minutes, until reduced by half. Set aside. In a medium skillet over medium heat, melt the butter. Add the onion and garlic and cook for about 5 minutes, stirring occasionally, until the onion is soft. Add the flour and mix well. Cook for 2 minutes, stirring once. Add the reduced beef broth

continued on next page . . .

. . . continued

and mix well. Add the horseradish, chili sauce, and pepper and mix well. Bring to a boil, reduce to a simmer, and cook for 3 minutes. Transfer to a bowl or a gravy boat and set aside. ❸ Prepare the grill for cooking over direct high heat. Place the steaks directly on the cooking grate. Cook for 4 minutes. Flip and cook for another 3 to 4 minutes for medium-rare, or to your desired degree of doneness. Remove to a platter and let rest for 4 minutes. Serve with the steak sauce on the side.

QUEEN OF STEAKS: FILET MIGNON STUFFED WITH BLUE CHEESE

SERVINGS

Filet mignon is the most tender of all steaks. It comes from the tenderloin muscle, which just doesn't do much work in its life, and that's a good thing for the cook. A filet typically isn't very well marbled either, but since it's tender, marbling's not very important. It's also a bit leaner for the health conscious, so that, too, is a good thing. Because of its lack of marbling, the filet mignon has a very mild flavor that pairs well with added flavorings like the blue cheese in this recipe. Topping a steak with blue cheese is a time-honored tradition, so why not stuff it inside? Just be sure not to overstuff it; and to squeeze the pocket closed, pushing the cheese in as far as possible so it stays in during the cooking. If a little runs out that's okay, it will just make it look better. These would go very well served with grilled portobellos and French fries or fried onions.

---

4 USDA Choice or better filet mignon steaks, about 2 inches thick

Big Bold Steak Spice (page 82), as needed

1 cup crumbled blue cheese

---

❶ Cut a deep pocket on the side of each of the steaks, with as small of an opening as possible. You might want to have the butcher do this for you. Stuff one-fourth of the blue cheese into the pocket of each steak. Work the cheese in as far as you can and squeeze the opening shut to seal it. ❷ Season the steaks liberally on both sides with the Big Bold Steak Spice. ❸ Prepare the grill for cooking over direct high heat. Place the steaks directly on the cooking grate. Cook for 3 minutes, rotate the steaks ¼ turn to make the nice crosshatch marks, and then cook for another 2 minutes. Flip and cook for another 3 to 4 minutes for medium-rare, or to your desired degree of doneness. Remove to a platter and let rest for 5 minutes before serving.

NEW YORK STEAK AU POIVRE WITH SHALLOT-COGNAC SAUCE

4
SERVINGS

This is a classic preparation for a New York strip steak. The coarsely cracked black pepper is pressed into the steak, and, while it seems like it may be too much, the flavors come together beautifully when cooked. The classic version includes a pan sauce made with the drippings but since we're grilling this one, the sauce starts with butter. The shallots and Cognac are typical, and when you taste the combination you'll understand why. The simplicity of this dish is what has made it timeless. Some things just don't need to be changed much. These would go very well served with garlic-infused mashed potatoes and a spinach salad.

4 New York strip steaks,
1½ inches thick

Salt

8 teaspoons coarsely
cracked black pepper

. . . . .

SHALLOT-COGNAC SAUCE

1 stick butter

1 cup finely chopped
shallots (about 10 shallots)

4 cloves garlic, crushed

Pinch of dried thyme leaves

1 cup Cognac

2 teaspoons flour

½ cup beef broth

❶ Season the steaks to your liking with salt on both sides. Press 1 teaspoon of the pepper into both side of the steaks. Set aside. ❷ To make the sauce: In a large skillet over medium heat, melt the butter. Add the shallots and garlic and cook for about 4 minutes, stirring occasionally, until the shallots are soft. Add the thyme and Cognac and cook for 2 minutes. Add the flour and mix well to smooth all the lumps. Cook for 2 minutes. Add the beef broth and cook for 2 minutes. Set aside and keep warm. ❸ Prepare the grill for cooking over direct high heat. Place the steaks directly on the cooking grate. Cook for 4 minutes. Flip and cook for 4 more minutes for medium-rare, or to your desired degree of doneness. Remove to a platter and let rest for 3 minutes. To serve, top each steak with one-fourth of the sauce.

CHILI-RUBBED RIB-EYE STEAKS WITH CILANTRO BUTTER

4

SERVINGS

The rib-eye steak is the favorite of many a meat eater. Marbling is what makes a steak juicy and tender, and the rib eye has more marbling than any other cut. If you prefer the boneless version go ahead and make the substitution here. I just prefer the flavor of any steak cooked on the bone. A chili powder–based wet rub goes on these steaks and it's a wonderful match with the rich taste of the beef. Be sure to get a good-quality chili powder. I like the San Antonio Red that I get from Pendery's, but there are many other good ones as well. When it comes to chili powder, it's best to look beyond the supermarket. Topping the chili-rubbed rib eye with the Cilantro Butter gives it a nice cooling feel in your mouth. These would go very well served with green chile cornbread and pinto beans.

CILANTRO BUTTER

2 teaspoons olive oil

½ cup finely chopped cilantro leaves

1 large shallot, minced

1 clove garlic, minced

Pinch of finely ground black pepper

1 stick of butter, at room temperature

CHILI RUB

4 tablespoons good-quality chili powder

2 tablespoons salt

1 teaspoon granulated garlic

1 teaspoon onion powder

1 teaspoon smoked paprika

⅓ cup olive oil

· · · · ·

4 USDA Choice or better bone-in rib-eye steaks, 1½ inches thick

❶ At least a few hours and up to 1 month before you plan to cook, make the butter. In a small skillet over medium heat, heat the oil. Add the cilantro, shallot, and garlic and cook for 2 to 3 minutes, stirring often, until the shallot is soft. Transfer to a bowl and set aside to cool. In a medium bowl, cream the butter with a fork. Add the cilantro mixture and blend well. Transfer to a 12-x-12-inch sheet of waxed paper and form into a log about 8 inches long in the center of the sheet. If the mixture is too warm to handle, just refrigerate for a couple of minutes until it is ready. Roll the butter up in the waxed paper to make a firm log and twist the ends to hold it tight. Place in the freezer until firm.

❷ One hour before you plan to cook, make the rub. In a small bowl, mix together the chili powder, salt, granulated garlic, onion powder, and smoked paprika. Add the oil and mix well. Place the steaks on a big platter and brush the wet chili rub evenly on both sides of the steaks. Refrigerate until it is time to cook. ❸ Prepare the grill for cooking over direct medium-high heat. Place the steaks directly over the cooking grate. Cook for 4 to 5 minutes per side for medium-rare, or to your desired degree of doneness. Remove to individual serving plates and top each steak with a couple of thin slices of the butter. Let rest for 5 minutes before serving.

SKILLET-FRIED TOP SIRLOIN

2

This is the way my Grandma Julia cooked steaks. I don't remember her ever going near the grill, but she didn't need to. She was from France and she regularly cooked steaks in the frying pan along with hand-cut fries made from red-skinned potatoes. I now know this as a fancy French restaurant dish called Steak Frites. The fancy French restaurants don't use red potatoes, but they may want to try it sometime. Grandma cooked her steaks in oleo, but I've switched that to butter and olive oil for you, although I still break out the margarine once in a while for old time's sake. The trick is to cook the steaks hot enough to get them nicely browned, but not so hot as to burn the drippings in the pan. Then, when you deglaze, and Grandma only did this with water, you get a nice, brown tasty *jus*. Cook it down to a very small amount and it will be rich and delicious. These would go very well served with fresh-cut red-skinned potato French fries and fresh corn on the cob with lots of butter.

92

Chapter 3: STEAKS

1 USDA Choice or better top sirloin steak, 1¼ inches thick

Steak Seasoning Salt (page 82), as needed

1 tablespoon butter

1 tablespoon vegetable oil

❶ Season the steak on both sides with the Steak Seasoning Salt. ❷ In a large skillet over medium-high heat, melt the butter along with the oil. When hot, add the steak and cook for 4 minutes or until well browned. Flip and cook for another 4 minutes for medium-rare, or to your desired degree of doneness. Remove the steak to a platter. Pour off as much fat as possible and discard. Add ¼ cup water to the pan and deglaze, scraping the little brown bits at the bottom of the pan and stirring to incorporate. Cook for 2 minutes, until the liquid is mostly gone. To serve, pour the drippings over the steak.

CITRUS-AND-SOY MARINATED FLANK STEAK

2

SERVINGS

This is a great recipe to take to a picnic or tailgate party. Just make up the marinade and get the steak soaking the night before, then take it to the party sealed up nicely in the zip-top bag—in a cooler, of course. Once you're at the party, you just grill it quickly, slice, and serve to the guests as part of a salad, in a wrap, or on a sandwich. It will help flavor any of these things wonderfully but, of course, it does equally well served on a plate as a steak dinner. The slashes that are made will help the appearance, as well as allow the marinade to penetrate a little better. Just don't make them too deep and remember that flank steak gets tough and dry if cooked beyond medium-rare. This would go very well served with rice pilaf and glazed carrots.

1 cup orange juice

½ cup soy sauce

5 cloves garlic, crushed

1 teaspoon finely ground black pepper

1 USDA Choice or better flank steak, about 1½ pounds

❶ In a small bowl, whisk together the orange juice, soy sauce, garlic, and pepper. With a sharp knife, cut a few shallow slashes into the steak on a 45-degree angle to the grain. Repeat in the other direction to form a grid pattern. Repeat the process on the other side. Put the steak in a heavy-duty zip-top bag and pour the marinade over it. Squeeze out as much air as possible and seal the bag. Turn the steak to coat all over. Cover with plastic wrap and refrigerate for at least 4 hours and up to 12 hours. ❷ Prepare the grill for cooking over direct high heat. Place the steak directly on the cooking grate. Cook for 4 minutes. Flip and cook for another 3 to 4 minutes for medium-rare. Remove to a platter and tent loosely with foil. Let rest for 5 minutes. To serve, thinly slice against the grain and on a 45-degree angle to the cutting board to create wide, thin slices.

FLAT-IRON STEAK WITH SAUTÉED MUSHROOMS

SERVINGS

The cut we know as the flat-iron steak has only been around for a short time, but it's quickly become a favorite among steak lovers. It's cut from the chuck and is second only to the filet mignon in tenderness, but has a great rich taste similar to a sirloin. It's made its way into most supermarkets and is typically priced to be a very good bargain. The sizes vary from 1 to 2 pounds, so you'll need to buy accordingly. The boneless steak, however, is easily cut into the serving-size pieces you'll need. I've topped the flat-iron steak with a tasty version of sautéed mushrooms that uses the earthy-tasting baby portobellos and a bit of red wine. I think the combination is perfect, but you could also use the mushrooms with just about any other cut of steak. These would go very well served with roasted new potatoes.

2 flat-iron steaks, about 2½ pounds total

Big Bold Steak Spice (page 82), as needed

• • • • •

SAUTÉED MUSHROOMS

2 tablespoons olive oil

1 pound baby portobellos, quartered

½ medium red onion, finely chopped

3 cloves garlic, crushed

½ teaspoon salt

¼ teaspoon finely ground black pepper

¼ teaspoon dried thyme leaves

½ cup red wine (you should be drinking the rest of the bottle)

❶ Cut the steaks in half and season liberally on both sides with the Big Bold Steak Spice. Refrigerate. ❷ In a large skillet over medium-high heat, heat the oil. Add the mushrooms, onion, and garlic and cook for about 8 minutes, stirring often, until the onion is soft. Add the salt, pepper, and thyme and mix well. Add the red wine and mix well. Cook for another 6 to 7 minutes, until the liquid is mostly evaporated and the mushrooms are tender. If more liquid is needed, add more wine. Keep warm on the stove. ❸ Prepare the grill for cooking over direct high heat. Place the steaks directly on the cooking grate. Cook for 4 minutes. Flip and cook for another 3 to 4 minutes for medium-rare, or to your desired degree of doneness. Remove to a platter and let rest for 3 minutes. To serve, spoon the mushrooms over the steaks.

SKIRT STEAK FAJITAS WITH FRESH PICO DE GALLO

SERVINGS

This is a classic Mexican restaurant dish, but instead of the typical sizzling grilled onions and peppers, I've added a homemade *pico de gallo*, which is just a fancy name for "salsa." The filet cutting of the steak makes it tender and it cooks really quickly. The flavor of the skirt steak coupled with the lime juice and the spicy fajita seasoning is what makes this dish great. Be sure to cut it thinly across the grain after cooking. This would go very well served with refried beans and Spanish rice.

PICO DE GALLO

One 10-ounce can diced tomatoes with green chiles, drained

¾ cup canned black beans, drained and rinsed

1 medium onion, chopped

2 jalapeños, seeded and finely chopped (leave the seeds in if you like more heat)

½ cup chopped cilantro

½ teaspoon salt

¼ teaspoon finely ground black pepper

Juice of 1 lime

FAJITA SEASONING

1 tablespoon salt

1 tablespoon good-quality chili powder

½ tablespoon finely ground black pepper

½ tablespoon granulated garlic

¼ teaspoon ground cumin

¼ teaspoon white pepper

Pinch of cayenne pepper

• • • • •

2 pounds skirt steak

1 lime, cut in half

10 eight-inch flour tortillas

❶ To make the *pico de gallo*: Put the tomatoes, beans, onion, jalapeños, and cilantro in a large bowl. Mix well. Add the salt, pepper, and lime juice. Mix well and set aside. ❷ To make the fajita seasoning: Add the salt, chili powder, pepper, granulated garlic, cumin, white pepper, and cayenne to a small bowl. Mix well and set aside. ❸ With a long, thin sharp knife, filet the steak into two thinner steaks by holding the meat down on a cutting board and cutting through it. Cut the steaks into 6-inch pieces. Squeeze half of the lime on the meat, and then season liberally with the fajita seasoning. Flip the meat and repeat. ❹ Prepare the grill for cooking over direct high heat. Place the steaks directly on the cooking grate. Cook for 3 minutes. Flip and cook for 3 more minutes. Remove to a platter and let rest for 3 minutes. Warm the tortillas in the microwave for 1 minute. Meanwhile, slice the steaks thinly against the grain. Mix the *pico de gallo* well, again. Divide the meat evenly among the tortillas and let the guests add the *pico de gallo*.

MRS. RICE'S PEPPER STEAK

6

This is a dish I've been eating for a very long time. As far back as I can remember, my best friend in life has been Mike Rice. Mike's mom is Mrs. Rice. This is how she makes her pepper steak and, since hers is the first I ever ate, it's how I like it and how I make mine. She generously shared the recipe with me about twenty-five years ago, and I've kept it ever since. It's always served with white rice, and Mike always made those pop-in-the-can crescent rolls with it to help soak up the gravy. So when I make this recipe, I always make those rolls with it, too. I think you'll like the combination and you'll wish Mrs. Rice were your friend. These would go very well served with white rice and crescent rolls.

One 28-ounce can whole peeled tomatoes, juices reserved

1½ pounds round steak, about ½ inch thick

½ cup flour

½ teaspoon salt

½ teaspoon finely ground black pepper

¼ cup vegetable oil

1¾ cups water, plus ½ cup if needed

½ cup chopped onion

1 clove garlic, crushed

1 tablespoon beef gravy base

½ tablespoon Worcestershire sauce

2 large green bell peppers, cut into ½-inch strips

❶ Cut the tomatoes into ½-inch-thick slices and transfer them to a bowl, saving any juice together with the reserved juices. Cut the round steak into ½-inch-wide strips about 2 inches long. Combine the flour, salt, and pepper in a pie plate. Mix well. ❷ In a Dutch oven over medium-high heat, heat the oil. Dredge the strips of round steak in the flour mixture until well coated and add them to the pan. Cook the strips, turning occasionally, until they are golden brown. Drain off as much of the oil as possible. Add the reserved tomato juices, the 1¾ cups water, onion, garlic, and gravy base. Mix well. Bring to a boil, reduce to a simmer, and cook for 1 hour, stirring occasionally. Add the tomatoes, Worcestershire sauce, and bell peppers and mix well. If the mixture seems too dry, add another ½ cup of water now. Return to a simmer. Cover and cook for another 45 minutes, until the meat is tender. Remove the lid and cook for another 5 minutes, or until the sauce is thickened.

ST. LOUIS–STYLE BARBECUE PORK STEAKS

4

SERVINGS

This is the signature barbecue dish of St. Louis. When you go to the grocery store there you'll be amazed how many pork steaks are in the cooler. Everybody loves them. Pork steaks are really just slices of the pork butt, and they cook up very well on the grill. But in St. Louis, they get a very unique treatment after the grilling. I think you'll like it. In St. Louis, the overwhelming favorite barbecue sauce is Maul's, and it's very good. If you want the authentic version and Maul's isn't available locally, be sure to order some online ahead of time. These would go very well served with baked potatoes and fresh sweet corn.

---

4 pork steaks, ¾ inch thick

Rib Rub #99 (page 21), as needed

2 cups your favorite barbecue sauce

---

❶ Season the pork steaks liberally on both sides with the Rib Rub #99. Prepare the grill for cooking over direct medium heat. Place the pork steaks directly on the cooking grate. Cook for 5 minutes. Flip and cook for another 5 minutes, or until golden brown on both sides.

❷ Remove the pork steaks from the grill and reduce the heat to medium low. Lay the pork steaks in a 9-x-12-inch disposable aluminum-foil pan, halfway overlapping each other. Pour the barbecue sauce over the pork steaks, spreading the sauce to cover them completely. Cover the pan tightly with aluminum foil and return to the grill.

❸ Cook for 30 minutes and check for doneness. The pork steaks should be very tender. Add a little water, if needed, and cook longer to your desired degree of doneness. To serve, remove the steaks to a platter and pour the sauce into a bowl to be served on the side.

SEARED TUNA STEAKS WITH WASABI BUTTER

4 SERVINGS

My friend Chris Capell of the Dizzy Pig BBQ Company served me this dish one day and I liked it so much that he offered to share his original version for this book. "The seared crust provides a beautiful burst of flavor, then the mellow tender fish comes in underneath. The whole experience is rounded out by the wild combination of butter and wasabi. Like all fish dishes, this one depends on the freshest of fish, and the hottest of fires. The key is to blast a quick crust onto the tuna without cooking the center too much. Think sushi. The center should be raw." These would go very well served with an Asian-inspired slaw and some spicy black beans.

RUB

2 teaspoons kosher salt

1 teaspoon freshly ground black pepper

1 teaspoon granulated garlic

• • • • •

4 fresh ahi tuna steaks, 1¼ inches thick

WASABI BUTTER

1 stick butter

4 scallions, chopped

½ teaspoon fresh grated ginger

2 tablespoons soy sauce

1 tablespoon plus 1 teaspoon rice vinegar

2 teaspoons sesame oil

1 tablespoon plus 1 teaspoon wasabi powder mixed with 2 tablespoons water

❶ To make the rub: Add the salt, pepper, and granulated garlic to a small bowl. Mix well. Season the fish evenly on both sides with the rub. Let rest for at least 5 minutes. ❷ Prepare the grill for cooking over direct high heat. Place the tuna directly on the cooking grate. Cook for 1 to 2 minutes, just until the tuna is charred. Flip the tuna and cook for another 1 to 2 minutes, until charred. Remove to a platter. ❸ To prepare the butter: In a medium saucepan over medium heat, melt the butter. Add the scallions and ginger and cook for 2 minutes, stirring occasionally. Add the soy sauce, vinegar, sesame oil, and the wasabi mixture. Mix well. ❹ To serve, transfer each tuna steak to individual plates and top with one-fourth of the butter.

CHAPTER 4

WINGS

ONCE UPON A TIME ALL CHICKEN WINGS WERE COOKED WHILE ATTACHED TO THE REST OF THE CHICKEN OR SERVED AS THE

scrawny part of a chicken dinner. But that was until one historic Friday night in 1964 at Anchor Bar in Buffalo, New York. That's the night when Teressa Bellisimo cooked the first Buffalo chicken wings. It seems that Teressa's son, Dominic, was tending bar that night when a group of his friends came in looking for something to eat. Teressa had the notion to deep-fry the chicken wings and then toss them in a spicy hot sauce. They've been serving them at Anchor Bar the same way ever since. That's it. End of story. Unlike many food lore stories, this one is undisputed. Anchor Bar now sells many hundreds of wings every day, and their sauce is available in bottles all over the world. If you're ever near Buffalo, you really should go to Anchor Bar. It's like returning to the motherland of chicken wingdom. To sit at the bar and realize that it really all started here is quite a thrill for a foodie. The original Buffalo wings have also inspired other chefs to create endless spinoff versions, some similar and some radically different. It seems that Teressa not only created a great dish, she also showed the world that chicken wings can be cooked and sauced with just about anything that tastes good to create a winning dish. We all owe her a great deal of thanks. My first recipe here uses what is rumored to have been the original Buffalo wing sauce, but whether or not it is doesn't really matter. It's mighty tasty. But I've also given you some interesting alternatives to the traditional hot wing such as the Raspberry–Honey Mustard Wings and the Sesame-Teriyaki Chicken Wings. There are a couple of extreme variations as well. I think you'll be surprised by how good the Peanut Butter and Jelly Chicken Wings are. And who wouldn't like Bacon-Wrapped Chicken Wings? Last, but certainly not least, you'll find the Turkey Wings Parmigiana. They're quite different from Teressa's wings, but a delicious distant cousin that owes her thanks.

BUYING THE WINGS

There really aren't many choices when buying fresh chicken wings. You may find an all-natural brand that you like, but they don't usually offer just wings and when they do the wings tend to be small. I prefer medium to large wings because they simply have more meat on them. I like to buy whole fresh wings instead of the frozen cut wing segments. It seems like a convenience not to have to cut them, but when you're cooking a lot of them, flipping each one can be a lot of work. I also think the fresh wings taste better.

PREPARING THE WINGS

To prepare big, whole fresh chicken wings, cut the tips off and save them for stock. Then, slash the skin on the inside of the elbow joint, but don't cut them all the way through. This allows the wing to cook a little quicker and makes it easy to break apart after cooking if you want to. If you're serving a big crowd, you can break them apart to create more portions, but usually I serve them left intact. The guests can easily part them after I've slashed that joint for them. After they're cut, season the wings liberally with a wing rub, or just salt and pepper, and let them rest to soak the rub in for at least 15 minutes and up to 4 hours.

COOKING THE WINGS

The original Buffalo wings were deep-fried. I love them fried, but I usually reserve eating them that way for when I'm dining out. Deep-frying at home is kind of a hassle, so I usually cook my wings on the grill. I typically lay them directly on the cooking grate, but once in a while I use a hanging wing rack that's made specifically for cooking wings on the grill. It does a nice job of cooking the wings evenly and I can leave it unattended, but the downside is they take longer to cook that way. Chicken wings do well baked in the oven, too, but that char taste from grilling makes it my favorite method. All of the chicken wing recipes here call for grilling, but you can substitute by cooking them in the oven at 375 degrees F for 45 minutes. And if you do like to deep-fry at home, go for it. I'd suggest cooking the wings per the fryer manufacturer's instructions.

COOKING TIMES FOR CHICKEN WINGS

The cooking times for chicken wings will vary wildly depending on the size wings you choose and whether you cook them whole or in segments. I've estimated a direct grilling time of 25 minutes for most of the recipes here, but your times may be different. Your grill will have a big effect on the cooking time, as well, and we can't even use a thermometer to check them because it would be impossible to find a thick enough piece of meat to test. So, you're going to have to use your best judgment, and when you think they're looking good, break one open and check. When a wing is properly cooked, the skin should be golden brown and slightly crispy and the meat should be white with clear running juices.

SEASONING THE WINGS

Now that you have your wings ready and a plan for grilling them, you'll need to season them up! I've given you a tasty wing rub below and I call for it in most of the recipes here, but you could use any of the rubs from the other chapters in its place. Chicken wings go well with just about any seasoning. You could even use simple salt and pepper if you like. You can sauce the wings while they cook. I usually toss them with the sauce after they come off the grill because it's easier, and that way the sauce doesn't burn. And besides, that's how Teressa did it with her original recipe. I've given you some really interesting sauces here, but there are many good ones available commercially as well. Mix and match and make the wings your own.

CHICKEN WING DRY RUB
MAKES ABOUT ¾ CUP

2 tablespoons salt	2 teaspoons good-quality chili powder
2 tablespoons Sugar In The Raw	2 teaspoons finely ground black pepper
2 tablespoons granulated garlic	1 teaspoon lemon pepper
2 tablespoons onion powder	1 teaspoon ground cumin
2 tablespoons paprika	¼ teaspoon cayenne pepper

Mix together and store in an airtight container.

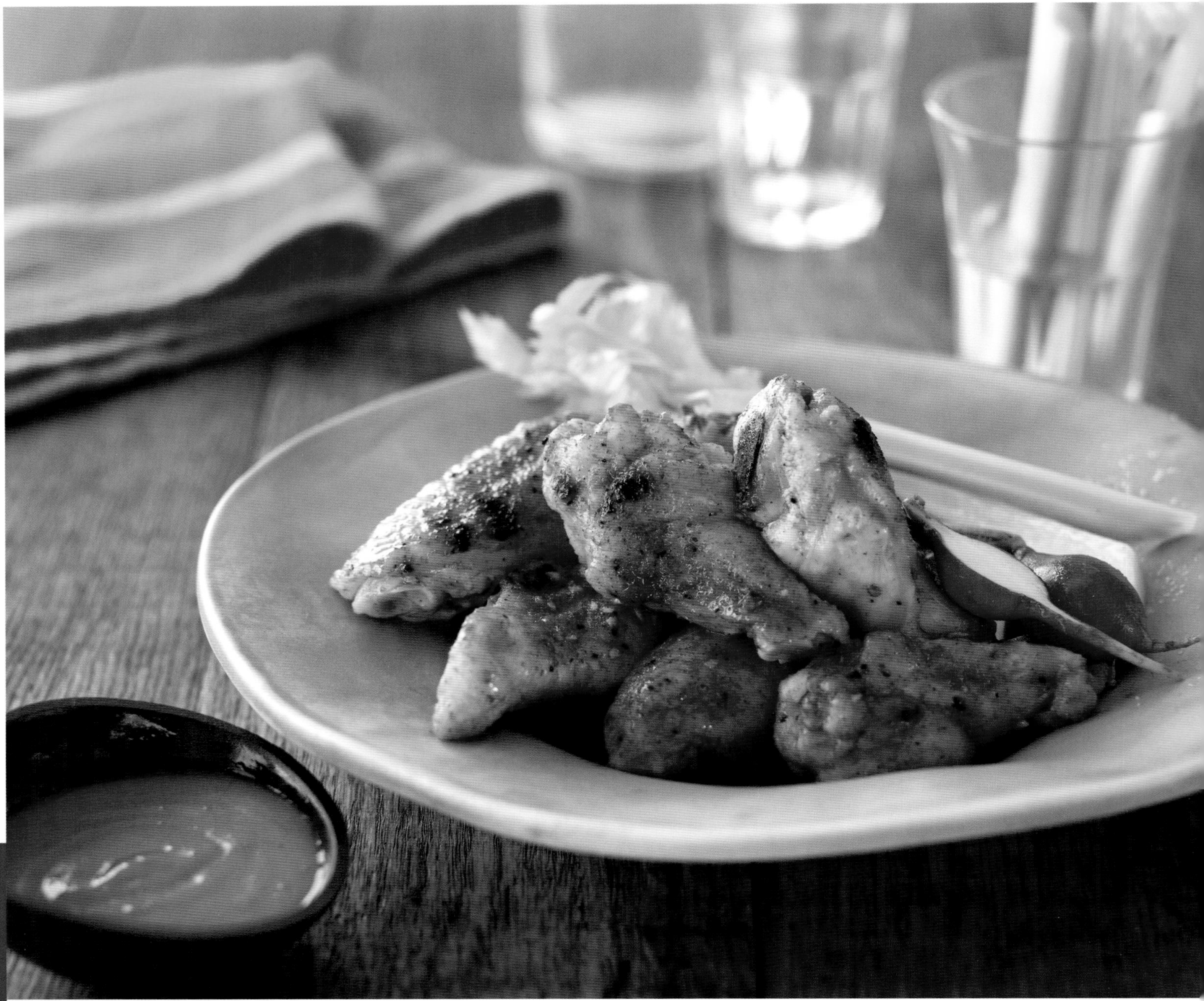

GRILLED HOT WINGS

10 SERVINGS

This is my very basic hot wing. This combination of simple ingredients is rumored to be the same as the original that was served that Friday night in 1964 at Anchor Bar. I wasn't there so I can't say for sure, but I can tell you that this is a good recipe that makes great hot wings. Frank's Red Hot sauce is readily available and very tasty, but it's not crazy hot. If you like them hotter, you might want to consider a more exotic hot sauce made with habañeros, but be careful because many people won't be able to eat them if they're too hot. These would go very well served with celery sticks, radishes, and blue cheese dressing.

10 fresh whole chicken wings

Chicken Wing Dry Rub (page 105), as needed

¾ cup Frank's Red Hot sauce

½ stick butter, melted

❶ With a sharp knife, cut the tips off the chicken wings and save them for stock. Slash the inside of the wing joint to help them cook more evenly, but don't cut them all the way through. Sprinkle liberally with the Chicken Wing Dry Rub. ❷ Prepare the grill for cooking over direct medium heat. Grill the wings for about 25 minutes, turning often. The wings are done when they are nicely browned and the juices run clear. Remove the wings to a platter. You may serve the wings whole but if you'd prefer to serve them in individual segments, cut them apart now. ❸ Whisk together Frank's Red Hot sauce and the butter. Transfer the wings to a large bowl. Pour the hot sauce and butter mixture over the wings. Toss to coat well. Transfer to a platter to serve.

DRY-RUBBED CHICKEN WINGS WITH RÉMOULADE DIPPING SAUCE

SERVINGS

These wings are cooked simply with the dry rub and served that way. I happen to like them just that way, but many of my friends prefer a sauce of some kind so I've made this Rémoulade Dipping Sauce to serve on the side. This mayo-based rémoulade is similar to the ones served with shrimp cocktail in New Orleans, but also resembles sauces typically served with fried chicken strips throughout the United States. This version isn't very spicy, but feel free to add a chopped jalapeño or some additional hot sauce, if you'd like it hotter. These would go very well served with French fries—and don't be afraid to dip the fries in the rémoulade, too.

10 fresh whole chicken wings

Chicken Wing Dry Rub (page 105), as needed

RÉMOULADE DIPPING SAUCE

1 cup mayonnaise

¼ cup prepared chili sauce

¼ cup sweet pickle relish

½ teaspoon hot sauce

¼ teaspoon dried tarragon leaves

❶ With a sharp knife, cut the tips off the chicken wings and save them for stock. Slash the inside of the wing joint to help them cook more evenly, but don't cut them all the way through. Sprinkle liberally with the Chicken Wing Dry Rub. Set aside. ❷ To make the rémoulade: Put the mayonnaise, chili sauce, pickle relish, hot sauce, and tarragon in a medium bowl. Mix well. Cover and refrigerate. ❸ Prepare the grill for cooking over direct medium heat. Grill the wings for about 25 minutes, turning often. The wings are done when they are nicely browned and the juices run clear. Remove the wings to a platter. You may serve the wings whole, but if you'd prefer to serve them in individual segments, cut them apart now. To serve, transfer to a platter, with the rémoulade on the side for dipping.

PEANUT BUTTER AND JELLY CHICKEN WINGS

10
SERVINGS

I was a little afraid that people would think I'd lost my mind when I offered these to them, so I tried them with my family first. They were a big hit, but it was my brother-in-law eating all the leftovers the next day that made me figure I was onto something special. I've used raspberry jam for mine, but the possibilities are endless. Peach, apricot, orange marmalade, and jalapeño jelly all sound real good to me. I'm not sure about the classic grape or strawberry, but I'll probably try those out on my brother-in-law, as well, the next time I see him. These would go very well served with toast points and potato chips.

10 fresh whole chicken wings	**⅔ cup seedless raspberry jam**
Chicken Wing Dry Rub (page 105), as needed	**⅓ cup creamy peanut butter**
	½ tablespoon hot sauce

❶ With a sharp knife, cut the tips off the chicken wings and save them for stock. Slash the inside of the wing joint to help them cook more evenly, but don't cut them all the way through. Sprinkle liberally with the Chicken Wing Dry Rub. Set aside. ❷ In a small saucepan over low heat, warm the jam, peanut butter, and hot sauce for about 5 minutes, stirring often, until well blended. Keep warm. ❸ Prepare the grill for cooking over direct medium heat. Grill the wings for about 25 minutes, turning often. The wings are done when they are nicely browned and the juices run clear. Remove the wings to a platter. You may serve the wings whole, but if you'd prefer to serve them in individual segments, cut them apart now. Transfer the wings to a large bowl. Pour the peanut butter and jelly mix over the wings. Toss to coat well. Transfer to a platter to serve.

CHILI-LIME CHICKEN WINGS WITH CILANTRO DIPPING SALSA

SERVINGS

Good chili powder has such a wonderful taste. I'm really not a food snob when it comes to ingredients, but I draw the line at supermarket chili powder. It typically has extra salt, garlic powder, and cumin in it and the quality of the actual ground chiles is usually pretty poor. The difference is well worth the effort of ordering it online. Unless, of course, you're lucky enough to live in Texas or the Southwest where they understand chili powder, and good options are readily available. Once you've got the good chili powder, you'll be eating well when you match it up with fresh lime juice as I have for these wings. It's a spicy and tasty combination. Add the cooling of the Cilantro Dipping Salsa and your mouth will be rocking. These would go very well served with guacamole or a bowl of spicy chili and a cold beer.

continued on next page . . .

. . . continued

**CHILI-LIME
WET RUB**

¼ cup good-quality chili
powder

¼ cup olive oil

Juice of 1 lime

1 teaspoon granulated
garlic

½ teaspoon salt

½ teaspoon cayenne
pepper

▪ ▪ ▪ ▪ ▪

10 fresh whole chicken
wings

**CILANTRO DIPPING
SALSA**

2 stalks celery, coarsely
chopped

½ large green bell pepper,
coarsely chopped

1 medium onion, coarsely
chopped

1 cup coarsely chopped
cilantro leaves

1 clove garlic, crushed

2 tablespoons olive oil

Juice of 1 lime

½ teaspoon salt

¼ teaspoon finely ground
black pepper

¼ teaspoon dried mint
leaves

❶ To make the wet rub: Combine the chili powder, oil, lime juice, granulated garlic, salt, and cayenne in a medium bowl. Mix well. ❷ With a sharp knife, cut the tips off the chicken wings and save them for stock. Slash the inside of the wing joint to help them cook more evenly, but don't cut them all the way through. Put the wings in a large bowl and pour the wet rub over them. Mix well to coat evenly. Cover and refrigerate for at least 1 hour or up to 12 hours. ❸ To make the dipping salsa: Add the celery, bell pepper, onion, cilantro, garlic, oil, lime juice, salt, pepper, and mint to the pitcher of a blender. Pulse until the mixture begins to liquefy, then purée for about 1 minute, until smooth. Transfer to a bowl. Cover and refrigerate. ❹ Prepare the grill for cooking over direct medium heat. Grill the wings for about 25 minutes, turning often. The wings are done when they are nicely browned and the juices run clear. Remove the wings to a platter. You may serve the wings whole, but if you'd prefer to serve them in individual segments, cut them apart now. Serve the wings with the salsa on the side.

HONEY-BARBECUE CHICKEN WINGS

10

SERVINGS

I have to think that shortly after someone ate the first hot wings they envisioned a barbecued version. You'll find barbecued wings on most menus where hot wings are served. My wings are always grilled, anyway, so it's only natural that some end up with barbecue sauce on them. For this sauce I've added a good portion of honey to really sweeten things up. Honey is a great match with fried chicken and it enhances just about any barbecue sauce, so the result is a real winner. You can use the barbecue sauce from the Chops chapter (page 65) or your favorite bottled sauce. These would go very well served with fresh biscuits and a tangy coleslaw.

10 fresh whole chicken wings

Chicken Wing Dry Rub (page 105), as needed

1 cup your favorite barbecue sauce

¼ cup honey

❶ With a sharp knife, cut the tips off the chicken wings and save them for stock. Slash the inside of the wing joint to help them cook more evenly, but don't cut them all the way through. Sprinkle liberally with the Chicken Wing Dry Rub. ❷ Prepare the grill for cooking over direct medium heat. Grill the wings for about 25 minutes, turning often. The wings are done when they are nicely browned and the juices run clear. Remove the wings to a platter. You may serve the wings whole, but if you'd prefer to serve them in individual segments, cut them apart now. ❸ In a small saucepan over medium heat, warm the barbecue sauce and honey, stirring often just until well blended. Transfer the wings to a large bowl. Pour the honey-barbecue sauce over the wings. Toss to coat well. Transfer to a platter to serve.

RASPBERRY-HONEY MUSTARD CHICKEN WINGS

SERVINGS

Another classic on wing menus around the country is the honey-mustard version. I think the wings have made honey mustard famous because now it's used in dressings and dips that stretch far beyond the humble chicken wing. Chefs use fancy mustards with honey for their salads in fancy restaurants and, of course, honey mustard is the dipping-sauce choice of many a chicken-strip eater. For my honey mustard, I add a little raspberry jam to sweeten things up and give it a unique flavor. These would go very well served with a big plate of Tater Tots.

10 fresh whole chicken wings

Chicken Wing Dry Rub (page 105), as needed

· · · · ·

RASPBERRY-HONEY MUSTARD

¼ cup seedless raspberry jam

⅓ cup yellow mustard

⅓ cup Dijon mustard

¼ cup honey

❶ With a sharp knife, cut the tips off the chicken wings and save them for stock. Slash the inside of the wing joint to help them cook more evenly, but don't cut them all the way through. Sprinkle liberally with the Chicken Wing Dry Rub. Set aside. ❷ To make the mustard: In a small saucepan over low heat, melt the jam. Add the mustards and honey, and mix well. Set aside. ❸ Prepare the grill for cooking over direct medium heat. Grill the wings for about 25 minutes, turning often. The wings are done when they are nicely browned and the juices run clear. Remove the wings to a platter. You may serve the wings whole but if you'd prefer to serve them in individual segments, cut them apart now. Transfer the wings to a large bowl. Pour the raspberry–honey mustard over the wings. Toss to coat well. Transfer to a platter to serve.

SESAME-TERIYAKI CHICKEN WINGS

SERVINGS

I really like making my own teriyaki sauce. It's so simple and has such a fresh taste, but what I really like is that I can change the sauce to match the food I'm cooking, my guests' taste, or even my mood. For these wings, I've kept the teriyaki sauce kind of middle of the road, but adding extra garlic or sesame oil would work, too, and it would go well on just about anything; for some guests I might skip the fresh ginger and garlic to tone it down a little. For another twist, if I wanted to use it on a piece of salmon, I'd add a little more brown sugar or maybe a little honey. There are so many possibilities. This is one sauce that you really should taste instead of just measuring it the way I did it. You just may come up with something you like better than mine. These would go very well served with vegetable fried rice or grilled slices of fresh pineapple.

---

10 fresh whole chicken wings

Chicken Wing Dry Rub (page 105), as needed

• • • • •

SESAME-TERIYAKI SAUCE
½ cup soy sauce

½ cup brown sugar

1 tablespoon sesame oil

1 tablespoon rice vinegar

2 cloves garlic, crushed

1 teaspoon minced fresh ginger

¼ teaspoon finely ground black pepper

• • • • •

3 scallions, cut on a diagonal

---

❶ With a sharp knife, cut the tips off the chicken wings and save them for stock. Slash the inside of the wing joint to help them cook more evenly, but don't cut them all the way through. Sprinkle liberally with the Chicken Wing Dry Rub. Set aside. ❷ To make the sauce: Mix the soy sauce and brown sugar together in a medium microwave-safe bowl. Add the oil, rice vinegar, garlic, ginger, and pepper. Mix well. Microwave on high for 1 minute. Stir, and microwave on high for another 30 seconds. Set aside.

continued on next page . . .

. . . continued

❸ Prepare the grill for cooking over direct medium heat. Grill the wings for about 25 minutes, turning often. The wings are done when they are nicely browned and the juices run clear. Remove the wings to a platter. You may serve the wings whole, but if you'd prefer to serve them in individual segments, cut them apart now. Transfer the wings to a large bowl. Pour the sauce over the wings. Toss to coat well. To serve, transfer to a platter and top with the scallions.

BACON-WRAPPED CHICKEN WINGS

10
SERVINGS

The thing that amazes me about this recipe is that I got to this point in my life without thinking of it before. It's just a natural for the grilling carnivore because, as we all know, everything tastes better wrapped in bacon. So you simply straighten out the chicken wing, wrap it in bacon, and cook it slowly until the bacon is cooked. Magically, the wing is done perfectly at the same time—like some kind of cosmic convergence. Makes you think that these two meats were meant to be together and we just never figured it out before. For me, just a little pepper is all they need, but if you'd like to brush them with a little barbecue sauce during the last few minutes or splash a little hot sauce on before eating, I think either would work well. It would be hard to do anything that would hurt this wonderful combination. These would go very well served with deviled eggs and steak fries.

10 fresh whole chicken wings

10 slices of thinly sliced bacon

Finely ground black pepper, as needed

❶ Soak 20 toothpicks in water for at least 1 hour. ❷ With a sharp knife, cut the tips off the chicken wings and save them for stock. Slash the inside of the wing joint to help them cook more evenly, but don't cut them all the way through. Straighten the wings and wrap each wing with a slice of bacon starting at the top and spiraling to the bottom. Secure with the toothpicks. Season the bacon-wrapped wings liberally with the pepper. ❸ Prepare the grill for cooking over indirect heat. Grill the wings for 30 minutes. Flip and cook for another 30 minutes, until the bacon is crispy and the wings are fully cooked. Remove the wings to a platter and let rest for 5 minutes. You may serve the wings whole, but if you'd prefer to serve them in individual segments, cut them apart now, taking care to keep the bacon in place. Remove the toothpicks and serve.

GRECIAN CHICKEN WINGS

SERVINGS

Growing up in Chicago, it seemed to me that many of the diners had Greek cooks and they often served a dish called Grecian Chicken. I don't know if this is an authentic dish from Greece or a Chicago-grown tradition, but I do know that it tastes really good. It's pretty simple, just roasted chicken topped with lots of garlic, olive oil, lemon juice, and a bit of oregano. It seemed like a natural to make a grilled wing version, and it worked out very well. This treatment works equally well with other parts of the chicken; just be sure to adjust your cooking time as needed. These would go very well served with rice pilaf and garlic bread.

10 fresh whole chicken wings

Chicken Wing Dry Rub (page 105), as needed

· · · · ·

GRECIAN WING SAUCE
½ stick butter

½ cup olive oil

6 cloves garlic, crushed

Juice of 2 lemons

Zest of 1 lemon

1 teaspoon dried oregano

½ teaspoon finely ground black pepper

Pinch of salt

❶ With a sharp knife, cut the tips off the chicken wings and save them for stock. Slash the inside of the wing joint to help them cook more evenly, but don't cut them all the way through. Sprinkle liberally with the Chicken Wing Dry Rub. Set aside. ❷ To make the sauce: In a medium saucepan over medium heat, melt the butter. Add the oil and garlic and cook for 4 minutes, stirring often. Remove from the heat and add the lemon juice, lemon zest, oregano, pepper, and salt. Set aside. ❸ Prepare the grill for cooking over direct medium heat. Grill the wings for about 25 minutes, turning often. The wings are done when they are nicely browned and the juices run clear. Remove the wings to a platter. You may serve the wings whole but if you'd prefer to serve them in individual segments, cut them apart now. Transfer the wings to a large bowl. Quickly bring the sauce back up to a simmer. Drizzle over the wings. Toss to coat well. Transfer to a platter to serve.

PIG WINGS

12

Anyone who ever declared that they would do something "when pigs fly" . . . well, you're still safe. These aren't actually pig wings, but they sure are good! I'm always looking for an excuse to eat more pork, and it seemed that there were plenty of chicken wing recipes here, so I created the pig wing. It's really just a big, thick, boneless pork chop cut into three strips, then soaked in a hot-sauce marinade, grilled, and glazed with barbecue sauce. You could use these new pig wings in any of the other wing recipes if you like. They'd even work in the bacon-wrapped wing recipe. Wow! Bacon-wrapped pig wings. The options are endless. Have fun with pig wings. These would go very well served with French fries and corn on the cob or a fresh green salad.

4 boneless pork loin chops, 1¼ inches thick	1 cup your favorite barbecue sauce
½ cup hot sauce	¼ cup honey

❶ At least 4 hours before you plan to grill the "pig wings," cut each pork chop into three long strips. Place the strips in a zip-top bag and pour the hot sauce over them. Seal and refrigerate for at least 4 hours and up to 12 hours. ❷ In a small saucepan over medium heat, warm the barbecue sauce and honey, stirring often, just until well blended. Set aside. ❸ Prepare the grill for cooking over direct medium-high heat. Remove the pig wings from the marinade and grill them for 2 minutes. Flip, and brush with the honey-barbecue sauce. Cook for 2 more minutes. Flip and brush with the sauce. Flip and brush often, cooking for another 3 to 4 minutes for slightly pink and juicy, or to your desired degree of doneness. Transfer to a platter to serve.

TURKEY WINGS PARMIGIANA

SERVINGS

Turkey wings are always there in the meat case looking good, but without a lot of exciting recipes for them. I sometimes roast or smoke them and they taste good, but they're never something I'd make for company. But these are different. They're tender and juicy and loaded with flavor from the browning and the baking with the marinara. The two-cheese topping puts them over the edge. The long neglected turkey wings are going to have a whole different look to you when you see them in the meat case after you try these. These would go very well served with *mostaccioli* and garlic bread.

1½ cups flour

1 tablespoon salt

2 teaspoons finely ground black pepper

4 whole turkey wings, cut into segments (reserve tips for another use)

1½ cups vegetable oil

One 24-ounce jar marinara sauce (I like Newman's Own)

2 cups shredded mozzarella cheese

½ cup Parmesan cheese

❶ Preheat the oven to 350 degrees F. Place the flour, salt, and pepper in a large zip-top bag and shake to mix well. Add the wing segments 2 or 3 at a time and shake well until coated. Remove and transfer to a baking sheet fitted with a rack. ❷ Heat the oil in a large, deep skillet until hot. Add the wing segments 4 at a time and cook for about 4 minutes per side, until golden brown. Transfer to the baking sheet with the draining rack to hold. Repeat with the remaining wings. ❸ Place all the wings in a pan large enough to hold them in one layer. Pour the marinara sauce over the wings, covering them evenly. Cover tightly with aluminum foil and bake for 1 hour. Remove the foil and top the wings evenly with the mozzarella cheese. Top that with an even layer of the Parmesan. Return to the oven for 10 minutes, until the cheese is hot and bubbly. To serve, transfer one of each type of segment to each of four plates. You can spoon the remaining sauce over precooked pasta.

WHERE TO GET IT

Anchor Bar Original Buffalo Wing Sauce
www.anchorbar.com

Big Green Egg
www.biggreenegg.com

Dried chiles
www.melissaguerra.com

Dr. BBQ
www.drbbq.com

Fiery Foods
www.fiery-foods.com

Fresh and interesting barbecue rubs
www.dizzypigbbq.com

Great barbecue sauce and rub
www.headcountry.com

Great chili powder
www.penderys.com

Great gas grills
www.napoleongrills.com

Great Sonoma Zinfandel
www.seghesio.com

The Greenbrier
www.greenbrier.com

Honey, barbecue rub, and other excellent products for the cook
www.buttrub.com

Hot sauces, wing sauces, barbecue sauces, and dry rubs
www.peppers.com

Prime steaks
www.allenbrothers.com

Rendezvous ribs and dry rub
www.hogsfly.com

Rib rack, wing rack, barbecue sauces, rubs, and tools
www.hawgeyesbbq.com

Sugar In The Raw
www.sugarintheraw.com

Steen's Cane Syrup
www.steensyrup.com

TABLE OF EQUIVALENTS

The exact equivalents in the following tables have been rounded for convenience.

LIQUID/DRY MEASUREMENTS

U.S.	Metric
¼ teaspoon	1.25 milliliters
½ teaspoon	2.5 milliliters
1 teaspoon	5 milliliters
1 tablespoon (3 teaspoons)	15 milliliters
1 fluid ounce (2 tablespoons)	30 milliliters
¼ cup	60 milliliters
⅓ cup	80 milliliters
½ cup	120 milliliters
1 cup	240 milliliters
1 pint (2 cups)	480 milliliters
1 quart (4 cups, 32 ounces)	960 milliliters
1 gallon (4 quarts)	3.84 liters
1 ounce (by weight)	28 grams
1 pound	448 grams
2.2 pounds	1 kilogram

LENGTHS

U.S.	Metric
⅛ inch	3 millimeters
¼ inch	6 millimeters
½ inch	12 millimeters
1 inch	2.5 centimeters

OVEN TEMPERATURES

Fahrenheit	Celsius	Gas
250	120	½
275	140	1
300	150	2
325	160	3
350	180	4
375	190	5
400	200	6
425	220	7
450	230	8
475	240	9
500	260	10